TEACHING LITERATURE IN HIGH SCHOOL: THE NOVEL

Standards Consensus Series

National Council of Teachers of English
1111 W. Kenyon Road, Urbana, Illinois 61801-1096

Production Editor: Jamie Hutchinson

Series Cover Design and Interior Design: Joellen Bryant

NCTE Stock Number 52821-3050

It is the policy of NCTE in its journals and other publications to provide a forum for the open discussion of ideas concerning the content and the teaching of English and the language arts. Publicity accorded to any particular point of view does not imply endorsement by the Executive Committee, the Board of Directors, or the membership at large, except in announcements of policy, where such endorsement is clearly specified.

Library of Congress Cataloging-in-Publication Data

Teaching literature in high school: the novel.
     p.   cm. — (Standards consensus series)
  ISBN 0-8141-5282-1 (pbk.)
    1. Literature—Study and teaching (Secondary) I. National Council of Teachers of English. II. Series.
  PN59.T42 1995
  807'.1'273—dc20   95-40689
                                         CIP

CONTENTS

7. Emphasis: Modern American Novels

INTRODUCTION

RATIONALE FOR THE STANDARDS CONSENSUS SERIES

Much attention is given to matters that divide the teaching profession. But when NCTE collected dozens of standards statements, curriculum frameworks, and other key state curriculum documents in order to prepare *State of the States—A Report on English Language Arts Content Standards in Each State,* considerable agreement was evident in many areas of English language arts instruction. Similar consensus has been demonstrated in the development of *The NCTE/IRA Standards for the English Language Arts,* the core document that outlines national standards in our discipline.

A heartening fact has emerged from the standards movement, as varied as that movement has been: We are after all a community of teachers who draw upon shared instructional traditions in literature, composition, language, and related areas. Furthermore, in recent years the insight and invention of teachers and teacher educators have built upon those traditions in fascinating ways. The result is a rich body of practice-oriented material that parallels the mounting consensus in the profession.

NCTE has developed the Standards Consensus Series, then, in recognition of the existence of core beliefs about the English language arts as revealed in innumerable standards-related documents and classroom ideas generated by teachers. The assumption underlying the series—and illustrated in it—is that good teachers have long been carrying out English language arts programs and classroom activities that exemplify sound implementation of the commonly held standards. The contents of each volume in the Standards Consensus Series were selected mainly from a database of classroom-practice materials. The database materials had been selected by teachers from a larger body of writings previously published by NCTE, mainly in the popular *NOTES Plus* journal.

In this volume we have gathered exciting activities that draw students into the wider worlds created in literature. The high value that our profession places on such encounters is plain from the sampling of standards documents quoted below:

> *South Carolina*—Students become familiar with the rich cultural heritage of language through experiences with

literature. By reading and personally responding to a variety of genres, the learner develops into a lifelong and selective reader who enjoys a wide variety of literature. (15–16)

Colorado—Students read and recognize literature as an expression of human experience. (4)

Michigan—Students will explore and respond meaningfully to classic and contemporary literature and other texts from many cultures that have been recognized for their quality and/or literary merit. (25)

Massachusetts—Students connect literature to personal experience and contemporary issues. (67)

Alabama—Students will demonstrate knowledge of the types, periods, and characteristics of literature from diverse cultures and places. (n.p.)

North Dakota—The students analyze the ways in which specific pieces of literature have been influenced by the culture and time period; understand that the reader interacts with the text; understand how genre characteristics affect a given text. (31)

Arkansas—[Students will] read excellent works and authors from various genres and cultures; analyze how the works of a given period reflect historical events; understand the relationship between contemporary writing and past literary traditions; develop criteria for judging the quality of literary works. (5)

New York—Students learn a wide variety of literary concepts commonly used in reporting on and discussing literature, including genre (poetry, novel, drama, biography, fable, myth, legend), plot, setting, character, point of view, theme, meter, rhyme scheme, tragedy, and comedy. (22)

Alaska—Students will use . . . literature of many types and cultures . . . to understand self and others. (n.p.)

These varied and powerful expressions of belief in the importance of literature point to the usefulness of this collection of materials on the novel as a key volume in the Standards Consensus Series. Of course, this is not to suggest that this book is of value only to those seeking to establish relationships between standards and instructional practice. Every high school teacher of the English language arts will find a wealth of lively, academically well-grounded ideas in this volume. Even if there had been no "standards movement" as such, these materials would nonetheless present a profile of exemplary practice worthy of emulation in improving students' performance in the English language arts.

Materials on exemplary practice in the teaching of the novel are especially important at the high school level. The novel is a complex literary genre. It is one that can afford enjoyment that will lead to lifelong reading habits. It deals with abiding themes and key issues that have been concerns of humanity through the ages. It can evoke crisp personal responses from students and generate thoughtful interaction in small-group and whole-class discussion. It can stimulate sustained analysis and critical and imaginative thinking. The novel is frequently a gateway to research—not only in the academic sense but in the broader sense of intensive inquiry into the forms of literature and life. For these reasons, the study of the novel was selected as the first literature-based volume in the Standards Consensus Series.

A few comments are in order about the nature of the materials and their organization. Consistent with NCTE position statements and with the texts of many standards documents, most of the classroom practices here do not isolate the teaching of literature as if it were unrelated to the entire range of English language arts skills and topics. The materials in the Standards Consensus Series demonstrate amply that good teachers often do everything at once—asking students to reflect on and talk about literary experiences, encouraging them to make notes about their readings and discussions in preparation for writing, and finding other ways to weave the language arts together in an integral learning experience.

A North Carolina goals document makes this point especially well: "Communication is an interactive process that brings together the communicator(s), the activity or task, and the situation that surrounds them. It is a constructive, dynamic process, not an isolated event or an assembly of a set of sub-skills. . . . Though listed separately, the [North Carolina] goals are not to be perceived as linear or isolated entities. The goals are interrelated aspects of the dynamic process of communication" (46). While the focus of this volume is mainly on teaching the novel, then, these classroom experiences typically exemplify the dynamics of real teaching.

ORGANIZATION OF THIS BOOK

The materials in *Teaching Literature in High School: The Novel* are grouped in useful ways that will be described below. However, neither the details of a particular classroom experience nor the arrangement of materials in this text is intended to be prescriptive. The day of know-all, tell-all books is past. Student populations differ; cookie-cutter activities simply don't work in every classroom environment. Most significant, teachers know their own students and have sound intuitions about the kinds of ideas and materials that are and are not appropriate in their classrooms. From this solid collection of materials, teachers are invited to select, discard, amplify, adapt, and integrate ideas in light of the students they work with and know.

The first four sections of this volume focus largely on approaches that usually have wide applications in teaching the novel. **Section 1— Emphasis: Components of the Novel** begins with "Literary Concepts Come Down from Their Pedestals." Typical of materials in this section, it is aimed at familiarizing students with such basic components as character, theme, and setting. Subsequent entries are devoted to other components—e.g., plot, tone, and style—always with the recognition that these are more than mere elements waiting to be uncovered in the text. Rather, they are powerful analytical tools that students can use to advantage as they encounter a rich, sometimes daunting genre.

Section 2—Emphasis: Responding to the Novel incorporates a variety of ideas for prompting student *participation* in the world of the text. The initial activities, such as "Recording Responses," "Literature Journals," "Lacing Literature through Life," and "Correlating Experiential Writing with Assigned Fiction," are geared toward opening the pleasures of the novel to young readers. Students are invited to write about novels in the comfortable space of their personal journals and to relate the works to their own experiences. Later entries encourage response through small- and large-group discussion and more formal writing assignments.

In succeeding sections, the entries move from the world of the text to the world *beyond* the text. **Section 3—Emphasis: The Novel, Media, and the Arts** and **Section 4—Emphasis: The Novel and the World** contain activities that connect the novel with, among other things, popular media and hot-button social issues. The materials in these sections are tilted toward relevance, but there is no lack of rigor here. Indeed, "Willa Cather and Georgia O'Keeffe: Exploring the Texts of Two American Artists" demonstrates how tandem readings of visual and verbal images can not only deepen students' appreciation of two great American artists, but also invigorate the teacher and help to revitalize the syllabus. "Ethics Questionnaire for Students" and "Looking at Freedoms in Literature" invite sober reflection on student attitudes as well as on literary texts and the wider world reflected in those texts.

Teaching Literature in High School: The Novel concludes with three sections on teaching *specific* novels: **Section 5—Emphasis: British Novels; Section 6—Emphasis: Nineteenth-Century American Novels;** and **Section 7—Emphasis: Modern American Novels.** Some of the entries describe approaches that are profitably applied to a variety of works (for example, "Allusions in *The Mayor of Casterbridge*"). But in most cases the value of these ideas lies in their special suitability to certain texts. For example, the *Hard Times* entry contains an extraordinarily rich array of prompts, assignments, and projects on the Dickens masterpiece. "Homer According to Morrison" points out what, for students and teachers alike, will be surprising and provocative connections between a contemporary African American classic, Toni Morrison's *Song of Solomon,* and a founding text of the traditional canon, Homer's *Odyssey.*

The preparation of this volume revealed that many topics and concerns found in NCTE's previously published classroom practice materials on the novel closely parallel the foci of the state-level standards statements cited earlier in this introduction. In a time of considerable pessimism and discord in education, it is encouraging to find such grounds for consensus in the teaching of the English language arts. In the emerging state and national standards, we find *common goals* for the teaching of our discipline. In the reported practices of the English language arts teaching community, we find *a formidable body of ideas about how to achieve those goals.* The Standards Consensus Series is both a recognition of cohesiveness and a tool for growth in the profession.

Finally, some acknowledgments are in order. First, kudos to the teachers and teacher educators who contributed their thoughtful practices to this collection, mostly via past issues of NCTE's *NOTES Plus.* The texts from that periodical are virtually unchanged, and the institutional affiliations of the teachers reflect their teaching assignments at the time of original publication. Issues of *NOTES Plus* and many other high school publications have been regularly reviewed by chairs of the NCTE Secondary Section. These include the present chair, Joan Naomi Steiner, and former chairs Mildred Miller, Jackie Swensson, Faith Schullstrom, George B. Shea, Jr., Theodore Hipple, and Skip Nicholson. Staff coordinators and advisors for *NOTES Plus* have also been a key in this endeavor. The staff coordinator since 1985 has been Felice Kaufmann. The teachers who categorized the vast body of materials for inclusion in NCTE's general database of teaching practices are Carol Snyder and Jim Forman. This text was compiled by NCTE staff editor Jamie Hutchinson.

REFERENCES

Alabama Department of Education. n.d. *Learning Goals and Performance Objectives.*

Alaska Department of Education. 1994. *Alaska Student Performance Standards.*

Arkansas Department of Education. 1993. *Arkansas English Language Arts Curriculum Framework.*

[Colorado] Standards and Assessment Council. December 1994. *Model Content Standards for Reading, Writing, Mathematics, Science, History, and Geography.* Final discussion draft.

Massachusetts Department of Education. March 1995. *English Language Arts Curriculum Content Chapter: Constructing and Conveying Meaning.* Draft.

Michigan State Board of Education. September 1994. *Core Curriculum Content Standards and Benchmarks for Academic Content Standards for English Language Arts.* Draft.

New York State Education Department. October 1994. *Curriculum, Instruction, and Assessment: Preliminary Draft Framework for English Language Arts.*

North Carolina Department of Public Instruction. 1992. *Competency-Based Curriculum. Teacher Handbook: Communication Skills, K-12.*

North Dakota Department of Public Instruction. 1994. *English Language Arts Curriculum Frameworks: Standards and Benchmarks.*

South Carolina English Language Arts Curriculum Framework Writing Team. February 1995. *English Language Arts Framework.* Field review draft.

1

EMPHASIS: COMPONENTS OF THE NOVEL

Plot, Character, Theme, Setting, Tone, and Style

LITERARY CONCEPTS COME DOWN FROM THEIR PEDESTALS

In my American literature classes, we often analyze what we've read in class according to literary elements and devices such as setting, tone, conflict, symbolism, and so on. The students do a good job of this, and some great class discussions have resulted.

I have always been happy with these discussions, but I've sometimes felt that students come away from the class with the notion that the literary concepts we study in relation to classic writing are not applicable anywhere else. With this in mind, I've adapted a teaching idea I first encountered when student teaching with Margaret Johnson of P. J. Jacobs Junior High in Stevens Point, Wisconsin.

In my version of this assignment, I explain to students that we will be going to the library and that each of them is to choose any novel that they would like to read. Students will have time both in and out of class to read, and after they are done reading, they will analyze their novels according to some of the literary elements we have discussed in class. As an added twist, students will contract to earn an "A," "B," or "C" for this assignment, depending on how much work they choose to do.

After we have visited the library and chosen books, I distribute copies of the previously studied literary elements in the form of a list of goals. (Other teachers may want to use their own lists; mine may be considered a starting point.)

It is important for students to understand that some literary elements, such as setting, tone, and conflict, are common to virtually all novels, while other elements, such as foreshadowing, symbolism, and irony, may be extremely important in some works and unimportant in others. Students will be better able to choose goals after they have done some reading in their novels.

I explain that in order to earn an "A," a student must select and meet five of the goals from the list; to earn a "B," he or she must meet four of the goals; to earn a "C," a student must meet three of the goals.

1. I can identify the theme of a novel. *I will state the theme of my chosen novel; then I will cite at least two examples which illustrate that theme.*
2. I can find reasons for the significance of a particular setting. *I will describe the setting in my novel and will list at least two reasons for the significance of that setting.*
3. I can compare a literary character's inner thoughts and feelings to his or her outward actions. *I will choose a character from my novel and list at least two comparisons between inner thoughts and feelings and outward actions.*
4. I can identify the point of view from which a novel is written. *I will list at least two passages that show the point of view from which my novel is written, and will tell why I think the author chose to use that point of view.*
5. I can interpret and critique the end of a book. *I will describe the end of my novel and will give two reasons for my belief that it is or is not credible or artistically justified.*
6. can recognize symbols and can tell what they represent. *I will list at least two symbols used in my novel and will tell what each one represents.*
7. I understand and can explain irony. *I will list and explain at least two examples of irony from my novel.*
8. I can tell if a work is satirical. *I will state at least two examples of satire and will explain what makes each one satire.*
9. I can point out types of conflict that arise in a story. *I will briefly explain two types of conflict that occur in my novel.*
10. I can recognize and interpret foreshadowing. *I will list at least two examples of foreshadowing from my novel, and will explain why I think the author chose to use foreshadowing in this way.*

I talk with students briefly about the list of goals before they begin reading; as they read, they may want to keep their eyes open for some of the particular literary elements and devices we have discussed. I emphasize that students are to *identify the literary element* as well as to *evaluate how well the author used that element.* For instance, when a student considers the novel's setting, he or she should describe the setting and try to judge how skillful the author was in creating the setting: "Does the author create a clear picture of the setting? How does the setting suit the novel's plot? Does it add anything to the mood of the novel ?"

For the next two days, students use class time to read. During this time, students who decide they do not like their novels may choose others. (I have found it wise to allow each student only one change, or the work does not get done.)

With their final selections chosen, students read and write in earnest, working sometimes in class and sometimes out of class. The time allotted for reading and writing can be adapted to the level of the students.

As students prepare this assignment, they know that they are free to come to me with questions, and they often revise what they've written as they work. Selected items from the finished writings may be read aloud by volunteers or by the teacher. This gives students a chance to learn how their peers recognized and evaluated conflict, character development, and so on in a variety of different novels. Such sharing also serves as a "teaser" to pique student interest in looking up some of the novels their classmates read.

I have used this assignment, with several variations, for five years, and have never failed to be pleased with the results. My students have chosen a wide variety of novels over the years, from *The Caine Mutiny* to *Pet Sematary*. Students enjoy the freedom of choosing their own novels, the literary elements that they want to explore, and the grade they want to earn. They come away from the reading, writing, and discussion in this activity with a better sense of how particular literary elements and devices are used, and of what makes good writing.

Jackie Pickett, New Auburn High School, New Auburn, Wisconsin

NOVEL NEWS

have used the project outlined below with *A Separate Peace*, *Lord of the Flies*, *The Scarlet Letter*, *1984*, and *The Adventures of Huckleberry Finn*. Every student in the class gets involved, and writing, speaking, listening, and organizational skills are practiced.

After the novel has been read, students work in small groups to prepare a thirty-minute news program based on incidents in the novel. There should be an anchor person or team, reporters, a weather forecaster, and a news analyst. Commercials and special interviews can serve a variety of purposes. Some reports can be broadcast directly from the scene; others may require the insights of outside experts.

Each group sketches out its segment of the program and prepares a written script that is passed in for approval. After the segments are sequenced, a period is spent videotaping the program and another is given over to viewing it.

As part of the evaluation, each student writes a letter to the network expressing positive and/or negative reactions to one or more portions of the program.

Evelyn Darden Floyd, Myers Park High School, Charlotte, North Carolina

SUPER SLEUTHS

In one of my assignments, my students take on the role of an investigating officer, taking a close look at a crime committed in a mystery novel that they have recently read. I use the activity in place of written reports on books read for a supplemental reading assignment. It would also be an appropriate assignment to substitute for reporting on a single book read in class. In addition, the activity is effective at a variety of grade and ability levels.

To set the mood for the activity, I invite a local police officer to talk to the students about the police reports that are prepared at the scene of a crime. The officer brings along appropriate forms for display and talks to the students about the need to investigate the crime scene thoroughly and to use clear and concise writing when filling out the forms. Then the officer interviews a student who takes on the role of one of the characters in the novel that he or she has read, demonstrating the type of questions that the police might ask as they investigate a crime.

At this point the students become the sleuths. I ask them to prepare a diagram of the scene of the crime, incorporating as many clues as they can supply. Next they fill out a Case/Incident Report form on which they present the statements of all the possible suspects in the crime. (You may wish to use the simplified version provided on page 8.)

Students might work in groups to supply the information for this form if several students have read the same novel or if it was a class assignment. Questions from someone unfamiliar with the novel can also add a new perspective to the gathering of pertinent information from the suspects.

Additional documentation might include a crime scene log, an evidence report, an evidence flow sheet, a request for examination of physical evidence, and an investigation mishap sheet. Students might pattern their forms after those used by the police department or devise their own.

My students have enjoyed this opportunity to respond to reading in a nontraditional manner. They also are exposed to the police as a resource other than as authoritarian figures, and they can better appreciate the role police play in criminal investigations. In addition, students are able to attempt a style of writing that is unfamiliar to them.

David G. Swift, Cheshire High School, Cheshire, Connecticut

Case/Incident Report				
Date of Incident		Day	Time of Incident	
Date of Report		Day	Time of Report	
Reporting Officer		Rank	Badge No.	
Type of Incident				
Suspects				
1)Name and Address		Sex	Weight	Height
Description				
Statement				
2) Name and Address		Sex	Weight	Height
Description				
Statement				
3) Name and Address		Sex	Weight	Height
Description				
Statement				
General Comments:				
This report is signed under the penalties provided by state law for making a false statement.				
Signed			Date	

STUDENT MAPS, CHARACTER MAPS

While reading *To Kill a Mockingbird* with my students, I came to the realization that, although the sequence of events and their importance were clear to me, my students were becoming lost in the lessons learned by Scout and Jem and the order in which they occurred. One of my primary thematic focuses in reading this novel was the growing up, or coming of age, of the Finch children. In order to help my students grasp this theme, I drew on an assignment I had discovered earlier in the year.

One day, as I was searching for new ideas the way most first-year teachers do, I went to consult with Margaret Palmer, a teacher known for her creative ideas and enjoyable lessons, and I immediately noticed the maps covering the walls.

"What in the world are those?" I asked.

"Maps of my students' lives. Aren't they wonderful?" she answered. My mind instantly began adapting the lesson to my purpose.

As a creative autobiography project, I decided to ask my students to design maps of their lives showing the major events thus far and the lessons, or growth, that resulted. I planned to ask each student to construct his or her map on a full sheet of poster board, just as I had seen in Mrs. Palmer's room. The first class day began a little roughly. I completely explained the assignment and then enthusiastically instructed the students to "Go to it!" Expecting to hear the sounds of frenzied writing, snipping, drawing, and other creative activities, I was deflated to hear dead silence. The students looked at me uncomfortably.

"Is there a problem?" I asked.

"Nothing exciting has ever happened to me," protested one student.

"I can't think of any major events in my life," added another.

Immediately seeing the problem, I picked up a piece of chalk and headed for the chalkboard.

"Let's brainstorm some ideas together! Well, let's see, a major event in my life was the birth of my baby sister," I began.

"Oh, yeah! I have two little brothers!"

"I have a brand-new nephew!" Students began writing.

"Another major event in my life was getting my first job," I continued. "How many of you have ever had a job?" Hands shot up around the room. More students began to write. "And then there was the day I got my driver's license," I said as I wrote on the board. Suddenly, there was a flood of responses, so many I could hardly keep up. They were on their way now. Students had illustrated such events as a divorce, the death of a friend or relative, misbehavior and its consequences, the first day of school, a trip to the dentist's office, family vacations, moving, first kisses, and so on. The second and third days were spent constructing maps. On the fourth day, students hung the maps around the room and then presented and explained their maps. The results were wonderful. I was thrilled to see the creativity of my students emerge. One student drew all of the different states she had lived in, illustrating the major events that took place in each state. Another student used a coffee can to trace circles in different places on the poster board and illustrated her events within each circle, connecting them chronologically with a road. Still another student drew a geographical map of the small town where he grew up and enlarged the locations of major events. Whatever the techniques he or she chose, each student's final product resembled a map, and the events were linked together chronologically. Under each illustration, which might be a photograph, a magazine cutout, a drawing, or any kind of creative visual, there was a brief description of the event and the change or lesson it provided.

Remembering the tactile, visual, and creative success of this assignment, I applied this lesson to Scout and Jem in *To Kill a Mockingbird*. I asked the students to map the life of one of these characters in the same way. As in the autobiographical map, each student illustrated and wrote about at least ten events in chronological order. This required students to search their book and notes for details and to draw conclusions based on personal opinion, class discussions, and information provided in the book. Again, the results were wonderful. We hung on the walls dozens of posters presenting the lives of Jem and Scout and the lessons they learned through experience. For example, one student mapped the highlights of Scout's life, like meeting "Boo" at last, and included bubbles showing Scout's thoughts about each of these events. Several students who mapped Jem's life included the time Jem found the knife in the oak tree, but each one handled it differently. One student sketched a picture of Jem finding the knife, while another showed just the knife on a timeline that included other significant items like his mended pants and Mrs. Dubose's white camellia. This lesson worked so well at helping the students organize the events in a character's life that I have begun to adapt it to other pieces of literature such as *Macbeth, Julius Caesar, Lord of the Flies, Beowulf,* and *The Odyssey.* The possibilities are endless. Thanks, Mrs. Palmer!

Lara Hutchinson, Samuel Clemens High School, San Antonio, Texas

THE GEOMETRY OF CHARACTER ANALYSIS

Geometry may sound like an unexpected partner for character analysis, but the two are well matched in the following strategy on characterization. By using geometric figures to represent characters and arranging them to suggest interrelationships, students can explore and discuss many possible interpretations of the personalities and situations portrayed in a novel.

Here's a list of steps to follow after students have read a novel.

1. Draw four or five simple geometric figures on the board (e.g., a rectangle, a circle, a triangle, an ellipse, a diamond).
2. Ask students, "What type of personality does each of these figures suggest?" On the chalkboard, record the adjectives and phrases suggested to describe each figure.
3. Name the main characters in the novel and ask students to decide which geometric figure best represents each main character. Record students' comments.
4. Ask students each to draw on a sheet of paper an arrangement of geometric figures that represents how the characters in the novel relate to one another. Encourage students to be creative in their arrangements and to use any means they can think of to express

the characters' interrelationships (e.g., connecting with arrows or with dotted or jagged lines, superimposing figures, varying shading, putting more or less distance between certain figures, and so on).

5. After ten or fifteen minutes, choose three volunteers to draw their diagrams on the chalkboard. Give the rest of the class a chance to try to interpret each diagram before its creator explains its intended meaning. If time allows, ask for additional volunteers, preferably students whose ideas differ markedly from those already presented.

6. For an in-class writing assignment, ask students to describe and explain their diagrams of the novel's characters and to back up their interpretations with specific details or passages.

7. For a homework assignment, ask students to use geometric figures to create a diagram that depicts the relationships in a television program, a movie, or an interaction in their own family or among their friends. These diagrams can be explained orally or in writing during the next class period.

Most recently I used these steps with Virginia Hamilton's *Sweet Whispers, Brother Rush* (Putnam, 1982). After students matched the main characters (Brother Rush, Dab, M'Vy, and Tree) with the figures I drew on the board (a square, a circle, a triangle, and an amorphous shape), they went on to devise many imaginative and provocative diagrams and explanations for the relationships among these characters. Shown below are three diagrams drawn by my students.

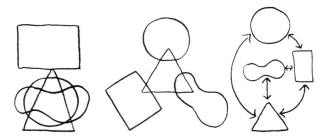

There aren't really any right or wrong interpretations in an exercise of this kind, which contributes to students' willingness to participate. The resulting discussions of character development help students better understand a novel's characters, relationships, and conflicts.

David Partenheimer, Northeast Missouri State University, Kirksville

A NEW LOOK AT CHARACTERIZATION PAPERS

One project my eleventh-grade American Literature students get involved in each year is the writing of literary analysis papers. Frequently, I begin the process with character analysis papers after we have finished a novel. Since the students are still developing their skills in analysis, they can sometimes benefit from practice in making inferences about characters and backing them up with textual examples. To make the writing easier for my students this year, I decided to try some prewriting exercises.

One day, borrowing from George Hillocks's "Spy Game" (from *Observing and Writing*, NCTE 1975), I brought a box of objects to class and spread them out on a desk. The box included ordinary things like car keys, ATM receipts, ticket stubs, and jewelry, as well as some more unusual items like a pie crimper, a protractor, a pipe, and a torn piece of paper with a phone number on it. In all there were about fifteen items. I invited the students to come look at the collection. After all the students had filed past the desk, I asked them to list all the items they remembered. Most of them did remarkably well on this part. Then I asked them what kind of person would carry these things around with them. I asked students to use their imaginations and to think of various reasons why a person might carry the given items. This suggestion helped students avoid stereotypical assumptions such as, for example, assuming that a person carrying a receipt for engineering textbooks must be a man, or assuming that a person carrying a lasagna recipe must be a woman.

A spirited discussion followed this question since everyone had a different idea about the person and why he or she had these things with them, often wonderfully original and creative ideas. Once a number of interpretations had been presented, I asked the students to write their own short stories about the characters they visualized, using at least ten of the items. The next day they enjoyed sharing their stories with each other. For the second prewriting exercise, I brought out a sack of bags—a handbag, a briefcase, a child's purse, a gym bag, a book bag, a jeweled evening bag, and a bag for a bike. I gave each group a bag and asked them to write a short description of the person who might carry it. After each group had seen about four bags, we shared observations.

Now that they had enjoyed working on these exercises, we were ready to start thinking about the characters from *The Scarlet Letter*, which we had just finished. Each group's next project was to write about the kind of bag a character from the novel might carry; in addition, they were to identify ten things in the bag that the character would carry. Of course, the group must be able to justify its choices by what had occurred in the novel. Much discussion occurred in the groups as they designed their bags and what would go inside—and the results were very detailed and imaginative. For instance, one group had Chillingworth carrying an expensive but worn leather doctor's bag that looked as if it had been singed by fire and had Indian signs carved in it. The same group put one of Dimmesdale's gloves (supposedly taken from the scaffold) in this bag. After we had shared our descriptions, we began to discuss what each of the items told us about the character. As the students made inferences, I made columns for the various characters on the board and started to list the person's characteristics. When we had finished our discussion we had new insights into the characters in the novel and a sense of how revealing textual details can be.

The final step was the students' writing of their own actual literary analysis papers. I allowed them to use the conclusions we had reached in class if they chose. Of course, they had to find the textual evidence to back their inferences up. As a result, the writing seemed to go more easily for the students, and all of my papers seemed to have more specific inferences and textual evidence than previous years. I hope their work with prewriting activities helped them accomplish this.

Janice McAuliffe, Mother McAuley Liberal Arts High School, Chicago, Illinois

TYING IT ALL TOGETHER

A few years ago I learned a game called "The Web of Life" from a biology teacher, and I adapted it to my students' study of *Great Expectations*. In this game, students are assigned characters to "become," and on the day we "tie it all together," they show the relationships among characters by constructing a web using a ball of twine. Although a character "web" is never the same neat, symmetrical item seen in nature, the process of creating it can be useful as a review session, as well as providing a visual comment on the complexity of character relationships within a novel.

Two or three days before the activity, I ask students to pick names of characters out of a bag; these are the "primary" characters. Students are asked to become as familiar as they can with their character by skimming the novel and talking about their character with other students. Students are allowed to trade characters, but we must know who is who the day before the activity.

On the day of the activity, the students wear large tags with their characters' names on them. We sit down and form a circle and I give the protagonist a ball of twine. (Sitting around a conference table is preferred, but the floor can be used also.) Holding one end, the protagonist chooses another character and throws the ball to him or her, first explaining a relationship between the two characters.

The student catching the twine holds onto the string and tosses the ball to a third student, again explaining a relationship between the two characters. Gradually, a web of relationships is formed. As the period draws to a close, I ask various characters to pull their strings. If the character is a major one, most of the students can feel the tension; if the character is a minor one, very few students can feel the tension.

It is important to suggest to students that they should not immediately throw the ball of twine back to the student who tossed it to them. For example, if Pip throws the twine to Joe, Joe should not throw it to Pip, but to another character, such as Pip's sister. Later, if a character such as Estella throws the twine to Joe, Joe may throw it to Pip. Of course, students are urged to toss the ball gently.

This game provides students with an excellent review of the novel's characters and plot. I have successfully used it studying other novels and plays containing many characters, such as *All Quiet on the Western Front*, *Brave New World*, and *Julius Caesar*. With smaller classes, the same activity has worked with *Of Mice and Men*, *Bless the Beasts and the Children*, and *The Old Man and the Sea*.

John Cebula, Glenbard West High School, Glen Ellyn, Illinois

THROUGH CHARACTERS' EYES

In this activity, students "become" one of the major characters in a book and describe themselves and other characters, using lists of accurate, powerful adjectives. The activity incorporates collaborative learning, vocabulary, and higher-level thinking on issues dealing with the text. The description below uses *The Scarlet Letter* as an example, but this activity is effective with any novel in which characterization is important.

After students have read a substantial portion of *The Scarlet Letter* and have discussed the relative strengths, weaknesses, and attributes of the various characters, divide the class into pairs. Give each pair a piece of butcher paper or newsprint (2' x 2' works well) and a wide marker. Instruct them as follows:

I want you to "become" one of the major characters from the book: Hester, Dimmesdale, Chillingworth, or Pearl. I want you, as that character, to list 10 adjectives that precisely describe each of the other major characters and 10 adjectives that precisely describe you. Write each list in a separate place on one side of your paper; don't put any names on the paper. Other groups will be asked to guess the character being described by each of your lists. Be sure to write legibly and in large letters, so that people can see your work from a distance. Remember that you "are" the character; each list, including the one in which you describe yourself, should reflect your experiences and prejudices. You may use dictionaries and thesauruses if you need them. Make your adjectives as accurate and precise as possible.

Give the students adequate work time (30-40 minutes) to compile their lists. Advise them to maintain secrecy, not to let others know who is being described in each of their lists. As they finish, post their work on the wall or blackboard until all lists are up. As students work, remind them that they are writing as their chosen characters, not as objective readers. Number the papers and assign each list a letter, so that everyone can refer to a particular list easily.

Each student pair then examines each list and, on a sheet of paper, attempts to identify who is being described.

Depending on the time available, the class then looks at each list or a selected number of lists, discussing identities. The authors of the lists under discussion finally give the "right" answers. Again, depending on time, the class can discuss the adjectives in each list and can cite specific events and details from the text which either support or call into question the accuracy of those adjectives. The class may also wish to look for patterns such as the number of pairs who chose a particular character, or adjectives that were repeated by several groups, as well as adjectives that did the best job of description.

John Forsyth, Park High School, McCleod Island, Livingston, Montana

WORDS THAT TELL TALES

Actions may speak louder than words, but words still speak loud enough to be revealing. The words spoken by a character in a novel are particularly telltale; if the author has chosen carefully, these words reveal just what he or she wants the reader to know about the speaker. In an exercise such as the following, quotations from a piece of fiction can be useful tools in studying characterization.

When I am teaching a novel such as *The Great Gatsby* or *A Tale of Two Cities*, I ask students to select from the book several quotations that reveal something about the personality of the main characters. The students then explain why they selected the quotations and talk about how important each quotation is to the development of that character.

Next, students have the chance to demonstrate their understanding of the various characters' personalities. I assemble all the quotations, type them, and reproduce them without revealing who the speaker is. Then I ask students to form four or five groups, and I give each group an envelope containing a full set of quotations to figure out. (And I make sure that I know the answers myself in case no one else does.) I usually suggest that each group member be responsible for one or two characters, so that by collecting passages that pertain to his or her character as they are identified, each person ends up with an organized collection of quotations at the end of the sorting process.

During this part of the exercise, interesting debates occur between students who are trying to determine who said what. Occasionally the more persuasive student is in the wrong, but the quotations and characters are finally straightened out when we all compare results. I actually count on these odd matchups, since they seem to be an effective way of provoking discussion of the author's craft.

Cindy Damon, Chelsea Public School, Chelsea, Vermont

THE DIFFERENT FACES OF LOVE

have yet to encounter freshman students who aren't fascinated by the whole notion of romantic love. Just like Romeo in William Shakespeare's *Romeo and Juliet,* they are constantly seeking a loving relationship with the guy or girl of their dreams or mourning the ending of a love gone wrong. But all too often, like Romeo, they find that love, which should create joy, produces instead feelings of sadness and loss.

In this unit, students are able to focus their attention on the topic which provokes so much interest—romantic love—and at the same time gain valuable insights into human nature and the dynamics of relationships. This is achieved through the in-depth study of the play *Romeo and Juliet* and of a contemporary young adult novel with similar themes. Several possibilities for comparison with *Romeo and Juliet* include *Ordinary People* by Judith Guest, *The Learning Tree* by Gordon Parks, and *Where'd You Get the Gun, Billy?* by Fran Arvick. I use my own young adult novel, *A Fine Line,* which has as its theme a possessive and abusive teenage relationship, and which I will use here to illustrate the implementation of the strategy.

The focus of the unit is on the motivation of the characters. Through an in-depth study of the main characters, students understand some of what propels each character into a destructive course of action. Students realize that the feelings of hopelessness exhibited by the characters are partly due to the limited options they see for themselves, and that these limitations are at least partly exaggerated by the characters' emotional state. Students can also see how lack of real communication with those around them contributes to the young people's problems. By the time students complete the response journals, Venn diagrams, character analysis charts, collages, and essays designed for this unit, students also begin to understand how many faces can be revealed in the name of love.

The unit begins with a brainstorming session on the topic: Can love ever be destructive? Students work in collaborative groups composing visuals that will be displayed in the classroom. They are asked to think of books, movies, plays, TV shows, and news events where tragedy or harm occurred as a consequence of love. After a class period to plan these collages and to set up a strategy to complete them, I suggest that they cut out pictures, headlines, news articles, and listings from TV guides at home and bring them in. They have time to work on them on Fridays after the weekly quiz covering the literature reading.

Next we discuss how characters are created. After the discussion, students create separate charts in their notebooks for each of the two couples we are studying. The headings on the charts are: *Author's description, Character's thoughts, Character's actions, Character's speeches*, and *What others say about him/her*. Throughout the reading of the play and novel, students fill in these charts with descriptive words, phrases, or quotations from the readings.

Some of the work in this unit is individual while other parts utilize collaborative groups. By the end of the unit, students have composed both creative and analytical writings as well as completed in-depth character studies. Nowhere are the students expected to reveal any confidential information nor are they placed in any awkward situations. I found, though, that many students came in to talk to me confidentially about "friends" who have experienced this problem. Some felt safe enough to disclose the fact that they have been involved in similar situations. They seemed relieved to find out that they were not alone. We begin by reading *Romeo and Juliet*, but before we read, students complete the following journal entry: *You are in love with a boy/girl your parents do not like. How do you plan to resolve this situation?* This will be the first entry in their response journals. The rest of the entries are formatted along the lines of an advice column. At least two times in each act, the students are to adopt the persona of Romeo or Juliet, the parents, the Nurse, Friar Laurence, or various other characters, and to write out a problem the character is facing, using facts from the play. Then students become the advice columnist and offer a solution to the problem. By the end of the play, students have completed a minimum of ten entries following this format.

Students now volunteer for a part to read. These parts change for each scene, so that all students get a chance to read the play aloud and to play the part of different characters. After a brief discussion about Shakespeare's language, students read Act I silently. The students reading parts are asked to focus on the meaning and emotions of the lines they will be presenting. The study of each act includes the following: silent reading, oral reading, and class discussion, using the questions at the end of each act as a jumping off point for analysis.

When we have completed reading and discussing *Romeo and Juliet*, we begin reading the contemporary novel, in our case, *A Fine Line*. In *A Fine Line*, students meet Maggie Garrity, a sixteen-year-old who is attempting to break away from a possessive and abusive relationship with her boyfriend, Tom Vaughn. Students are asked to complete their collages so that we can use them to initiate our discussion of when love can be destructive. This is a great topic to get students talking because many teens either have a "friend" who has been a victim of dating abuse or know someone who has been abusive. Also, with recent press and TV coverage of this problem, many students are aware of and are eager to discuss a topic that hits so close to home. Students start their journals for this segment by answering the following question: *You want to break off a possessive/abusive relationship, but your boyfriend/girlfriend doesn't want to let go. How do you resolve this dilemma?* The rest of the journals follow the same format used for *Romeo and Juliet*. This type of journal helps students to look at problems from the viewpoints of the differing characters, resulting in a clearer understanding of the many facets to a situation and expanding their usual way of perceiving a situation.

Although I started reading *A Fine Line* aloud to grab the students' interest, I found they enjoyed reading it silently better and then sharing exciting sections aloud in oral dialogues, with students joining together for the various dialogue sections. I assigned two chapters a night for discussion the next day, using the journals as a jumping-off point. Although I have compiled a list of factual and interpretive questions to go along with the chapters, other teachers who have used this unit prefer to focus on questions of their own choosing. Throughout our discussion, we refer back to the themes we discussed with the play: how obsession can lead to tragedy, how innocence can be destroyed when faced with the realities of life, and how lack of communication can lead to disaster. Students are constantly asked to compare and contrast the relationships, feelings, and actions of Romeo and Juliet with those of Maggie and Tom.

At this point, students are ready to complete Venn diagrams on the characters. I give them three copies of the intersecting circles. On one, they write the names of the two male protagonists—in our case, Romeo and Tom. Romeo's name goes above the left side of the circle and Tom's above the right side. Using their character analysis sheets as guidelines, students fill in the circles with words and phrases that describe the person. In the middle, where the circles intersect, they choose words and phrases that fit both of the characters. On the second sheet, they will follow the same directions for the female protagonists--in our case, Juliet and Maggie. The third sheet is for the parents: students write *the Capulets and Montagues* on one side and *Mrs. Garrity and Mr. Vaughn* on the other. My goal is to elicit a discussion revealing the similarities and differences between the sets of characters, leading into a discussion of how each of their personalities and values guide them to the actions they chose in the stories.

The unit is completed with a formal essay. Students pick one character and discuss questions such as, "How did a love which started out so joyfully become so destructive?" The essays are developed by covering the following points: What is one major change the character should have made? When should this have happened? What difference would this have made in the events that occurred? How would this change have led to a more positive outcome? Students are to use specific examples from the selections to support their points.

By the time students have completed this unit, they have a deeper understanding of human motivations, and they better comprehend how lovers can be blinded by words of love which effectively obscure clear thinking. Because love is a subject that enthralls teenagers, they enjoy playing the omniscient narrator, pointing out the bad decisions the characters make which lift them from the joys of love and drop them into a whirlpool of tragedy. As one student, a follower of Tina Turner, stated at the end of the unit, "What's love got to do with it?"

Constance Casserly, Herndon High School, Herndon, Virginia

TEAM PAPER

This year I decided to experiment with the group writing of research papers. After assurance from students that they were open to experimentation and a team effort, I listed five novels that would be read in the course: *Sister Carrie, The Red Badge of Courage, The Great Gatsby, A Separate Peace,* and *The Scarlet Letter.* The teams, five students each, selected a novel and began their research of the novel's historical period and locality. Before our library work began, we agreed to limit our sources to primary ones and made a long list of what one might want to know about a period and locality: major events, transportation, clothes, entertainment, government, religion, the arts, and so forth.

Problems, of course, developed when a team member was unprepared or absent, but students soon learned that a team effort involves cooperation, dependability, and accommodation. As they completed each step—outline, bibliography, footnote page, preliminary and revised drafts—students began to recognize that even when each one did a fair share of the work, there were times when someone had to lead or do extra work for the good of the group. Scheduling the typing of the final copy had all the excitement of a relay race! One group found itself retyping and proofing the final page of the paper during the lunch period before class.

I was impressed by the range and quality of the information students gathered in a short time and by the interest and enthusiasm they showed. Aside from the research skills they polished and the information they acquired—and shared with the entire class—students learned how to work with others to achieve a common goal. In their evaluations, students stated that although they now felt equipped to write a research paper on their own, they would find it more helpful and enjoyable to accomplish the task in a small group.

Joy B. Averett, Oxford, North Carolina

TAMPERING WITH TONE

Harper Lee's *To Kill a Mockingbird* is one of my favorite novels. Over the past few years, I have tried to develop accompanying activities that encourage improved reading, writing, and thinking skills. The activity described below is one that can help students at the secondary level recognize and understand tone and use it in writing.

I begin by reading aloud from the first chapter the line "Simon's stinginess was only exceeded by his piety." We discuss the connotations of *stinginess* and *piety* and identify Lee's tone. Then we change words in the sentence to change the tone to angry, sympathetic, satirical, and so on. An important part of our discussion involves noting how our impressions of the character and the author's attitude toward him or her would be affected if the passage had been worded differently.

Finally, we divide into groups of three or four to rewrite the passage using different tones. I suggest various possibilities and give students time to write. I may even create a few alternate versions of the passage myself. Later, we share our results; students read their passages aloud and discuss what they think the intended tone of a given passage is and why.

This activity has proven to be a very successful way of exploring tone. It's simple to adapt it for use with poetry, short stories, or other novels by varying the passages selected as models.

Helen M. Griffin, Mid-Carolina High School, Prosperity, South Carolina

FROM "FOR THE NONCE" TO "LIKE NOW"

Here's an activity that can be adapted to almost any pre-twentieth-century novel or play. It documents the timelessness of character and theme and enables students to break through the unfamiliar syntax of an earlier time.

Select a scene between a male and a female character critical to the novel or play. Identify your two best readers, one boy and one girl, and divide the remaining students into two groups of boys (Groups A and C) and two groups of girls (Groups B and D). Finally, choose three pieces of music for use as sound tracks--one classical, one modern and popular, one contemporary rock.

Before explaining anything about the activity, ask the two readers to prepare for the next day's class the dialogue as it appears in the text. After they leave to rehearse their lines, send Groups A, B, C, and D into the four corners of the room. Ask Group A to examine the male character's lines and to paraphrase each line into modern standard English; ask Group B to do the same for the lines of the female character. Then ask Groups C and D to follow the same procedure, converting the dialogue into modern English slang. Instruct each group to record its paraphrasings neatly enough so that one of its members, selected by the group, can present the rewritten lines in reenactments of the scene on the following day. While students spend the remainder of the period working in their groups, nose around, exercising a bit of editorial discretion here or suggesting a better word there—but only when asked.

On the next day bring along a tape or record player and the music you have chosen for soundtracks. Students will need about ten minutes at the beginning of class to make final alterations in their paraphrasings, but to preserve the spontaneity of real conversation, do not allow the readers from Groups A and B and from Groups C and D to rehearse. If possible, arrange the desks to resemble a theater and introduce the first pair of readers, who present the scene as it was originally written, accompanied by classical music. After the applause dies, set the stage for the next presentation—this one in modern standard English, with a popular modern melody in the background. Scattered laughter will undoubtedly make this reenactment longer than the previous one. After applause and giggles subside, introduce the last version, by far the noisiest and funniest version—modern English slang. The rock number with its driving beat adds grit to this rendition. At its conclusion, ask students what they learned not only about the literary work you are studying but also about the level of language.

Allan J. Ruter, Glenbrook South High School, Glenview, Illinois

From Hawthorne to Hemingway

AN EXERCISE IN STYLE

After my students have read the first two chapters of *The Scarlet Letter* (Signet Classic, 1980), I assign an exercise that gives students a chance to imitate Hawthorne's style. (Students will be even more ready for this assignment if they have also been introduced to several short stories that typify Hawthorne's themes and interests, such as "Young Goodman Brown," "The Minister's Black Veil," "Ethan Brand," and "Endicott and the Red Cross.")

I begin with some introductory notes about Hawthorne's style. To use a metaphor in keeping with the material, I like to tell students that Hawthorne uses phrasing "as elaborate as the embroidery of Hester's needlework." His "threads" as I list them for students are:

> words with Greek and Latin roots (some of his clear favorites are *lurid, physiognomy, retribution, malefactress, evanescent, impelled, ignominy*)
>
> archaic forms from the Elizabethan-Jacobean period appropriate to the stories about Puritans (such as *wottest, verily, prithee, sayest, hath, betwixt,* and *behoof*)
>
> litotes, or understatement, in which something is expressed by a negation of the contrary ("The age had not so much refinement that any sense of impropriety restrained the wearers of petticoat and farthingale from . . . wedging their not insubstantial persons . . . nearest to the scaffold at an execution." *The Scarlet Letter*, chapter 2, p. 58)
>
> subordinate clauses and parenthetical expressions ("It was a circumstance to be noted, on the summer morning when our story begins its course, that the women, of whom there were several in the crowd, appeared to take a peculiar interest in whatever penal infliction might be expected to ensue." *The Scarlet Letter*, chapter 2, p. 58)

As we talk about the types of language usage that make Hawthorne's style distinctive, students are welcome to find short examples in the text and to read them aloud to the class.

We then move on to a brief discussion of Hemingway's style. I suggest to students that Hemingway, in contrast to Hawthorne, represents the more familiar journalistic tradition in twentieth-century literature, his trademarks being sparse description, simple diction, minimal subordination, and direct phrasing. Again, I give students examples of these stylistic traits and allow any students who are interested to further illustrate points of style by reading passages aloud from a Hemingway text on hand.

Next, I explain the writing assignment. Students are to show an understanding of both styles by "translating" the content of one writer into the style of the other. I distribute selected passages in handout form (see page 29) and give students thirty minutes or more to write. The passages on the handout page are taken from *The Scarlet Letter* (Signet Classic, 1980) and *The Short Stories of Ernest Hemingway* (Scribners, 1939). Page references are as follows: #1: *The Scarlet Letter*, chapter 2, p. 58; #2: Ibid., chapter 6, p. 97; #3: Ibid., chapter 4, p. 78; #4: "Cross Country Snow," p. 188; #5: "Soldier's Home," p. 147; #6: "In Another Country," p. 267; #7: "My Old Man," p. 202.

It's not a bad idea for the teacher to tackle the "translation" process as well; it can be as stimulating a challenge to a teacher as it is to a student. When the translations are completed, they are shared and compared with the class, and we all join in the analysis of which passages and phrases best recreate the intended author's style.

Since many students become fairly adept with Hawthorne's style and enjoy recreating it, I give them another chance to practice it after we finish reading *The Scarlet Letter*. For students' final writing assignment on the novel, I offer them a choice between a more conventional thesis essay or one of the two creative scenarios that follow:

1. Year: 1660. You are a Puritan female in Boston, the wife (or unmarried sister—remember Mistress Hibbins!) of the governor. You are aware that the magistrates and ministers are discussing with great consternation a book published in England about an American Puritan adulteress. You are curious, although you know that *The Scarlet Letter* is a forbidden book until the officials can decide whether to censor it, or how to deal with it. You manage to obtain a copy of the book and, over a period of several days, while your husband is out, you read it. Write your response to it in the form of

journal entries or in the form of a letter to a close relative or friend in another community. (Obviously, the epilogue, chapter 24, would not be in a 1660 version" of the book.)

2. The time and place are the same as in the first scenario. You are one of the hoary-bearded magistrates involved in the judgement of the novel. In a letter, you convey your responses to a magistrate in another town, to apprise him of how the Boston eminences are dealing with the situation and what they are doing to safeguard the public.

I find that the majority of students choose to write on one of the creative scenarios. Furthermore, I am surprised at the number of boys that take the female's point of view and vice-versa. Perhaps students with the versatility to change writing style are better able to appreciate the challenge of a different gender role as well.

Rosemary Laughlin, University High School, Urbana, Illinois

AN EXERCISE IN STYLE

HAWTHORNE	HEMINGWAY
1. "There was, moreover, a boldness and rotundity of speech among these matrons, as most of them seemed to be, that would startle us at the present day, whether in respect to its purport or its volume of tone."	1.
2. "It was wonderful, the vast variety of forms into which she threw her intellect, with no continuity, indeed, but darting and dancing. Always in a state of preternatural activity, soon sinking down, as if exhausted by so rapid and feverish a tide of life, and succeeded by other shapes of similar wild energy."	2.
3. "Misshapen from my birth-hour, how could I delude myself with the idea that intellectual gifts might veil physical deformity in a young girl's fantasy!"	3.
4.	4. "They opened the door and went out. It was very cold. The snow had crusted hard. The road ran up the hill into the pine trees."
5.	5. "He liked to look at them, though. There were so many good-looking girls. Most of them had their hair cut short."
6.	6. "In the fall the war was always there, but we did not go to it anymore."
7.	7. "Gee, I could listen to my old man talk by the hour, especially when he'd had a couple or so of drinks."

2

EMPHASIS: RESPONDING TO THE NOVEL

Engaging the Text through Writing and Speaking

A TRIPLE
BRAINSTORMING
SESSION

One semester of sophomore English at Warren Township High School focuses on composition and the novel. Students read three core novels: *Lord of the Flies*, *A Separate Peace*, and *To Kill a Mockingbird*. Students also study composition as a process, so by the end of the semester they are familiar with brainstorming.

In this prewriting activity for an essay assignment, students brainstorm comparisons among *Lord of The Flies*, *A Separate Peace*, and *To Kill a Mockingbird*, considering what the children or adolescents in each novel learned through their experiences and what was most important to the characters in the stories. As students think and discuss, they note their ideas on a handout sheet that they may later refer to while they plan and draft their essays comparing the novels.

Our brainstorming session, conducted with the entire class contributing ideas, begins when I provide students with copies of the handout sheet. Under the heading, "A Comparison of Three Novels," the handout contains the three lists shown below. (I lay them out side by side, with space for responses after each item.)

Lord of the Flies
    List three to five of Ralph's characteristics.
    List three to five of Jack's characteristics.
    List three to five games or amusements of the boys.
    List three to five problems the boys face.
    List three to five lessons the boys learn.
    List the most important concerns of the boys.

A Separate Peace
> List three to five of Gene's characteristics.
> List three to five of Finny's characteristics.
> List three to five games or amusements of the boys.
> List three to five problems the boys face.
> List three to five lessons the boys learn.
> List the most important concerns of the boys.

To Kill a Mockingbird
> List three to five of Jem's characteristics.
> List three to five of Scout's characteristics.
> List three to five games or amusements of the children.
> List three to five problems the children face.
> List three to five lessons the children learn.
> List the most important concerns of the children.

The instructions on the handout suggest that students list three to five ideas in each category. Students are not limited to ideas generated during the brainstorming session, but can add more ideas as ideas occur to them.

Class discussion provides further development of the students' ideas about the novels. I ask students to think about what Jem, Gene, and Ralph have in common, and what Scout, Finny, and Jack have in common. I also ask them such questions as the following: "Do you recognize any of the traits listed in people around you? How do the characters help you to understand real life better? What do their activities have in common? What concerns do they share?" As we respond to these questions, I ask students to note the comments and ideas that interest them the most, so that they can come back to these later when deciding on a focal point for their essays.

By the time our brainstorming session is over, students have discussed many different comparisons and contrasts among the three novels, and have compared the notes they have taken on their handout sheets. Students generally have a lot of good ideas and are ready to plan their essays, in which they will select and compare some aspect of the three novels.

Jane Beem, Warren Township High School, Gurnee, Illinois

RECORDING RESPONSES

I use this assignment with *The Scarlet Letter*, but it could be used with almost any novel. I ask students to choose a particular character and write periodic journal entries as they read the novel, recording their responses and changes in their responses to that character. The journal entries are assigned as homework, and student volunteers can earn extra credit by reading their journal entries aloud to the class after we finish reading the novel.

After all students have finished reading, they meet in small groups to discuss their responses to the character they followed. Short reports of these discussions are made to the entire class at the end of the period.

Then students are ready to write reader-response papers in which they concentrate on the way their responses to the character changed over the course of the book, paying particular attention to the characterization devices employed by the author. I remind them to incorporate their journal entries and notes from the small group discussions.

Ellen Geisler, Madison, Ohio

LITERATURE JOURNALS

S tudent readers sometimes have difficulty understanding the words and actions of characters of differing ages, cultures, and backgrounds. To aid in bridging the gap in understanding, I use journals and assignments that encourage students to imagine themselves in the place of others. A diary, personal journal, or letter to a friend can provide the necessary vehicle for such expression. Here are three sample writing assignments I give to my students. I use the first two after students watch a videotape of the CBS film version of *Anna Karenina*. I use the third after students read *The Catcher in the Rye*.

Anna Karenina

1. As Anna, write diary entries to show your thoughts and feelings after at least five significant events in your life (e. g., on first meeting Vronsky, after telling your husband of your affair, or after agreeing never to see Seryozha again).
2. Selecting a particular point in the narrative, write journal passages that reveal the viewpoints and feelings of Karenin, then Anna, and finally Vronsky.

The Catcher in the Rye

1. Pretend that you are one of the following people: Stradlater, Mr. Spencer, Mrs. Morrow, Sunny, Maurice, Sally Hayes, Jane Gallagher, Carl Luce, one of the Lavender Room girls, the hat check girl, the cab driver, one of the nuns, Mr. Antolini, or D. B. Write journal entries describing one or more interactions you have

had with Holden Caulfield, describing your feelings and what you think of him.

Myron Bietz, Mayo High School, Rochester, Minnesota

LACING LITERATURE THROUGH LIFE

As part of the study of a novel, I often assign a series of short, daily writings that juxtapose events from the novel with the individual experiences of the reader. I suggest that students use "the lens of literature" to see and understand events in their own lives. These writings help students develop a deeper understanding of the emotions and actions of the novel's characters.

After discussion of a particular chapter or event in the novel, I distribute a list of three or four writing topics for the day. Students may write on one or all of the topics for a total of about fifteen minutes. The use of several topics gives students the option of avoiding topics that they might find too personal. Students are also free to write additional thoughts at home. I sometimes read aloud one or more passages related to the day's topics before asking students to begin writing.

The writing suggestions listed below are ones I use with *Wuthering Heights*.

1. Catherine kept dreaming she was in heaven and didn't belong there. Describe a dream that captured your attention after waking.

2. Catherine and Heathcliff were so anxious to leave the church that they could hardly sit still. Write about a time when you felt the same way.

3. Isabella had illusions about Heathcliff. Describe someone about whom you had illusions at some time, or describe someone else's illusions about you.

4. Heathcliff thrived on revenge. Write about a time when you were tempted to seek revenge or did seek revenge.

5. Nelly gave Heathcliff advice about reforming his heart. Write about a time when someone gave you advice about something important, or a time when you gave someone else advice.

6. Heathcliff usurped Hindley's father's affections. Write about a similar instance in your life or the life of someone you know.

7. Edgar took life as it came. Write about the attitudes and actions of someone you know who approaches life in a similar way.

8. Heathcliff believed his son Linton was worthless. Linton, too, came to believe that he was worthless. Explain how you have been influenced by another person's opinion of you.

9. Hareton's relationship with Cathy transformed him, bringing out the best in him. Explain what kinds of experiences bring out the best in you.

Mary Jo May, Henry Ford Community College, Dearborn, Michigan

CORRELATING EXPERIENTIAL WRITING WITH ASSIGNED FICTION

My students prefer an experiential involvement with the arts to a critical one. Here are some of the most successful assignments I have devised for use with works by Borges, Solzhenitsyn, and Baldwin. Not only were the assignments successful as examples of students' authentic voices but also as incentives to discussing criticism. Both selections and approach are geared toward older and better-prepared high school students.

Since the works of Jorge Luis Borges can be difficult to understand, I eased students into the abstract quality of his stories by first assigning them to read his essay, "Borges and Myself" (*Borges: A Reader*, E.P. Dutton, 1981). The essay begins:

> It's to the other man, to Borges, that things happen. I walk along the streets of Buenos Aires, stopping now and then—perhaps out of habit—to look at the arch of an old entranceway or a grillwork gate; of Borges I get news through the mail and glimpse his name among a committee of professors or in a dictionary of biography. (Borges, 278)

After reading this, I assigned students a one-page essay on the two sides of themselves: "artist and I" or "public and private I." When they finished writing, they were more than willing to share their results with the class, which helped us get to know each other better. Then we discussed both works—theirs and Borges's. At this point, students were ready for the ever-present duality of his work.

Next, we read Borges's story, "The Other Life," which was more difficult both to understand and to write about experientially. "The Other Life" is a story about a man who as a youth serves in a revolutionary army. In the final battle, he is cowardly, but he is reputed to have died in the act of bravery. Many years later, after leading a life of no distinction in a remote village, he dies.

I asked my students to think of an event in their lives or in the life of someone close to them that became with time fictionalized, distorted, or opposite to its original meaning. Some wrote about breaks in friendships or love relationships from the view of the rejected person, whose initial view is of course far different from the gilded one that comes years later. Some wrote of their parents' divorce from immediate and later points of view. While the students found "The Other Life" difficult at first, this assignment eased the way to a lively class discussion on duality in Borges's fiction.

Solzhenitsyn's *One Day in the Life of Ivan Denisovich* presented another type of challenge. Frankly, I sometimes tired of discussing it. So, instead, I asked students to take five sheets of paper and write a record of one day in life, choosing a recent day, infusing it with Ivan's philosophy as proof that they had read the book and understood Solzhenitsyn's point of view. I shaped the assignment further by asking students to set aside five sheets of paper. Each sheet was to be labelled Breakfast, Morning Activities, Afternoon Activities, Dinner, Bedtime. I directed students to write items on each sheet rather than fully develop each page in sequence. This was to avoid the usual last minute rush at the end. Students worked steadily the entire class session, writing sentences under each heading, flipping back and forth.

The results of this assignment were far better than I had envisioned. Students revealed an understanding of Ivan's attempts to make the best of everything—whether it was a moldy piece of bread saved for bedtime or building a brick wall under the pressure of being censored if late. Several wrote of disappointments culminating the day: one student found out her boyfriend had betrayed her with her best friend, another student realized that he could not continue his job because of a personality conflict with fellow workers. Uniformly they applied Solzhenitsyn's underlying spirit of counting their blessings and resisting despair.

After this writing assignment, my students were eager to discuss the novel, and questioned why the Soviet censors allowed the book to be published. They were repelled by the prison use of numbers instead of names and were anxious to examine subtle ways in which prisoner could turn against prisoner.

I used another experiential writing assignment in a course in which we were studying the stories of James Baldwin. I assigned Baldwin's "Previous Condition" along with a personal essay on students' experiences as a scapegoat or in scapegoating others. At first, students denied having experienced either. However, as we discussed further, they thought of situations that they could relate. One student wrote a humorous account of how his oldest brother made scapegoats of him and his four younger brothers. Through the humor, one could feel the frustrations of a powerless person. Another wrote of an experience akin to the film "My Bodyguard." (In the film, a slender, small, nonathletic boy seeks protection from a large hulking boy with a reputation as a bully.)

These assignments have proven so helpful to the students' understanding of fiction that I now create similar ones in other courses. They do not preclude reading the critics. Rather, they stimulate curiosity about the text and enhance understanding.

Lila Chalpin, Massachusetts College of Arts, Boston

NAME THAT CHAPTER!

Writing conventions, like styles in fashion, seem to change with the times. It occurred to me, after teaching works by Mark Twain and Charles Dickens, that modern writers such as J. D. Salinger, John Steinbeck, and Harper Lee do not give titles to individual chapters; they merely number them. An obvious explanation is that the earlier writers produced their work for serializing in magazines and newspapers.

The readers of these earlier works are given clues as to what to expect with such titles as "The Cat and the Painkiller," *(The Adventures of Tom Sawyer)* or "Monseigneur in the Country," *(A Tale of Two Cities)*, and can begin to make predictions based on these titles. Discussion about these novels can focus on what happened previously, what this particular chapter will bring that is new or suspenseful, and what the author's purpose or tone will be.

What, then, should be done with the novel that does not have chapter titles? Elementary! Name that chapter! I have made it a practice to generate chapter titles as we proceed through such works as *The Pearl* or *To Kill a Mockingbird*.

Students are asked to make a cumulative list as we proceed. At the beginning of class, sample titles are elicited and "tried out." Discussion follows on accuracy, word choice, and connotation. Does the chapter title offer a summary, identify a key item, "bait" the reader, or offer a bit of intrigue? Sometimes there is disagreement; sometimes there is embarrassment when students who have not read are quickly identified.

Here are some sample chapters for *To Kill a Mockingbird:* "Scout's Childhood" or "Knowing Maycomb" for chapter 1; "The Beginning of a Rough School Year" or "A Disastrous School Day" for chapter 2. Such titles immediately focus on the main idea or offer insight about particular events in the life of the Finch family.

Current research in reading emphasizes the interactive process. I like naming chapters because it is a means of placing responsibility on students. They must reflect on their reading, make decisions, choose words carefully and exactly, and be prepared to justify their responses. Chapter titles create immediate discussion and debate. Finally, the cumulative list makes it possible for the entire class or the individual student to review an entire novel, whether using the author's titles, as in the case of *A Tale of Two Cities*, or newly created titles, as in the case of *Catcher in the Rye*. "Name That Chapter!" can be a very useful technique for teaching and enriching reading in the secondary classroom.

Edith Broida, Oak Park High School, Oak Park, Michigan

DISCOVERIES THROUGH DIALOGUE

I've found a virtually surefire way to engage a complete class in an animated, teacherless discussion about a piece of literature.

I've used this assignment successfully with high school students and college sophomores, and, after I presented it in an inservice, a middle school teacher told me she had found it effective with her students as well. I invite students to write a dialogue between readers in disagreement, as preparation for discussing the literary work in class.

For a quick start, I write on the board opening speeches of two readers who have come to differing conclusions about an event or character central to the book's significance. One such pair of speeches sets up a *foolish/wise* dichotomy as a stimulus for thought. In a high school class, for example, after the students had finished reading *The Chosen*, by Chaim Potok, I wrote the following interchange on the board:

> "Wow! Danny Saunders has a fool for a father, doesn't he?"
> "What are you talking about? Reb Saunders is just about the
> wisest character in the book."

I told the students to continue the dialogue, writing until I stopped them. Then I sat down to write as well. After about twelve minutes, everyone had written more than a page and some much more. I said, "Bring your dialogue to a conclusion now, giving the last speech to the person who most nearly expresses your own estimate of Reb Saunders's behavior."

Students shared their dialogues with a neighbor and added, as postscripts to their own dialogues, any arguments they hadn't thought of before the exchange.

I asked for a show of hands to see how many ended their dialogues with the first speaker and how many with the second. Those in the first group moved to one side of the room and those in the second group to the other. "Now," I said, "tell your colleagues on the other side of the room why you gave the last speech to the first, or to the second, speaker."

From my neutral vantage point at the end of the room between the two groups, I was able to listen to a rousing debate on the character of Reb Saunders. The students didn't need my direction. Because they had written the arguments of both speakers, they were better prepared to respond to points raised by their classmates across the room. More students spoke, with greater conviction and with more factual supporting evidence, than in our typical class discussions. Their efforts to clarify their reactions explained the central significance of the book for them in ways my teacherly questions never do.

Mary Cobb, Western Washington University, Bellingham, Washington

POLL TALK

Literature discussions didn't always go well in my classes. Sometimes students had little to say; perhaps more frequently, a few students had *everything* to say. To spark better student interplay I came up with an idea that has served me well: the opinion poll.

After we finish reading a work of literature, I take an opinion poll in the form of a subjective true-false quiz. I tell students that they cannot be right or wrong and that their opinions certainly do not have to agree with mine. Then, usually in class, I ask them to clarify their judgments in writing. Writing nudges all students into some sort of opinion, and now it's easy to draw out even the most reticent students: "How about a show of hands of those who answered false to the first question? Ah, Cindy, tell us why you feel that way."

Since discussion of the answers to the poll often takes several days, I collect the polls. Sometimes I make tabulations. (For example, "All but three of you felt that 'false' was the best response to the third question.") Sometimes I make notes of an individual student's answers so I can draw that student out the next day. Sometimes I turn the poll into a writing assignment ("Pick one question about which you have a definite opinion and . . . "). Finally, I have on occasion written to the author of the work we have read and sent him or her the poll and its results. Of course this won't work with Shakespeare, but, for example, I had an excellent response from Joseph Heller about our *Catch-22* poll. Sharing Heller's responses with the class after we had completed our discussion led to a spirited discussion about an author's intention versus a reader's interpretation.

To characterize the nature of our literature polls I've appended five questions that are typical of the twenty-item poll for *Catch-22*.

1.	*Catch-22* is basically a pessimistic work.	T	F
2.	One major force behind Yossarian's running away at the end is his desire to help the other men.	T	F
3.	*Catch-22* was written out of hope--the hope that human beings would see their faults and start to improve.	T	F
4.	*Catch-22* is a sexist novel, blatantly unfair in its portrayal of women.	T	F
5.	The novel's criticisms of American society are now a bit out-of-date.	T	F

Samuel B. Pierson, The Loomis Chaffee School, Windsor, Connecticut

FROM RESPONSE TO CRITICISM

The phrase "interpretive community" appears more and more often in reading and composition literature for teachers. Junior and senior high school students may sometimes feel that they are denied the inner secrets of this literary "interpretive community." As one student claimed, "It's no fair! You know the theme and symbolism here because you have the teacher's book!" Teachers may need to put aside the teacher's book occasionally and see what happens when their students create meanings from texts and critique them from the viewpoint of their own interpretive community. We also learn from their points of view.

Step 1
Choose two or three short stories or poems or perhaps a few excerpts from a novel the class is reading. Tell the class that there is no teacher's manual (that you will not be using one) nor are there any preset answers or interpretations for these readings. The students' job is to respond to the readings in meaningful ways. Responding that "I liked or hated this story" is only *one* response: summarizing the story is only one response. They should come up with as many ways to respond as they can think of. No response is invalid, wrong, or stupid. Ask students to make a list of their responses.

Step 2
In small groups (3-5 students), students combine and create a master list of responses, adding comments as they come to mind in the group session. Each story or poem has its separate list of responses.

Step 3

Then ask each group to categorize their responses, giving names ("labels") to each category and creating a chart of categories and responses.

The chart that students create may look something like the one shown. (This sample chart should not be given to students beforehand, since it would prestructure responses.)

"THE ROAD NOT TAKEN"

CATEGORY   SPECIFIC STUDENT RESPONSES

REMINDS ME OF...

WHAT IT MEANS

HARD TO UNDERSTAND PARTS

IMAGES

THE ADVENTURES OF HUCKLEBERRY FINN

THEMES

TONE

ACTION WE LIKED

BORING PARTS

Remind students that their responses can be grouped into *various kinds or categories* of responding. Some students may use such formal terms as *theme, character, tone,* and so on for their category labels; others will make up their own labels, such as "boring parts," "reminds me of . . .," "what it means," and so on. You will need to move around the room suggesting groupings and encouraging students to rearrange their ideas and responses by category. It's all right to have a category with a single response in it.

Another group might happen to have a similar category, or the existence of the category might stimulate discussion.

Step 4

Each small group then reports to the class as the teacher and a few student helpers create a larger summary of responses. All of the categories are recorded, and tally marks are placed next to the category to show how many groups suggested that as a category. Some of the responses for each category are recorded, enough so that the category is clear.

The class is encouraged to see similarities and differences in the following:

> responses to each piece of literature across groups
> categories for each piece of literature across groups
> responses across pieces of literature
> categories across pieces of literature

Step 5

Finally, some discussion questions:

    a.   Why do we get similar responses?
    b.   How does one's background influence his or her responses to literature? If we all have similar backgrounds, will we all have similar responses?
    c.   What else besides background affects our responses?
    d.   What makes a community of readers?

e. People in an interpretive community don't always agree. Are there many differences of opinion in this class?

f. Where might the differences come from?

g. How can this activity and realization about ourselves help us as a group (a community)?

h. Are responses ever wrong? What makes them wrong?

i. What makes them right?

j. How do differing responses inform or enhance our understanding of what we read?

From here some teachers may want to talk about various kinds of literary criticism, showing students how close they come with their categories and responses to many well-known types of criticism.

The community that develops among students is the most positive outcome of this activity (which can be done many times with varying kinds of literature and writing, including their own). But the teacher learns, too. Teachers learn about important issues in the lives of their students; they watch the political and social interactions of individuals as they discuss, debate, and resolve interpretations; they learn how much students have already learned about academic/literary communities as they use terms like theme, symbols, analogy, and so on, depending on their level of academic sophistication. Teachers have an opportunity to follow up the lesson by making connections between what the students do and what literary critics do, thereby narrowing the gap between "us" and "them" that so many students quite legitimately feel.

Marti Singer, Georgia State University, Atlanta

AUTHOR NOTES

As a requirement for my American literature class, I ask students to keep a notebook of the usual lecture notes, literary terminology, quizzes, and homework assignments—and something extra. I ask them to include "author notes" for every author we read.

"Author notes" are details about the author, written on worksheets that I provide. Each worksheet is lined and divided into the following sections: full name of author, important facts or accomplishments, personality traits, characteristics of the author's style, titles and publication dates of four published works, famous quotations, and personal reaction.

I like students to learn a quotation that they are likely to hear again, preferably one from a major work that we have read. For this reason, I supply the first quotation from each author myself. I write the quotation on the chalkboard ahead of time and ask students to copy it onto their worksheets. Students are welcome to find and include additional well-known quotations by the same author.

Examples:

From Herman Melville's *Moby Dick*: "Call me Ishmael."
From Edgar Allen Poe's "The Tell-Tale Heart": "True!—nervous—very, very dreadfully nervous I had been and am: but why *will* you say that I am mad?'"

For the "personal reaction" section of the worksheet, I explain that students are to select a specific passage, character, description, or idea and react to it in two to three sentences. For example, one student responded to Emerson's "Nature" essay by writing, "When Emerson says, 'I become a transparent eyeball,' I know what he means. Sometimes when I'm out in the woods on a spring day, I feel so at one with nature that I imagine I can see every living thing and that they can see into me."

We complete the first author worksheet together after students read and take notes on the biographical information in their literature text. As the year progresses, students become skilled at ferreting out the necessary information and completing their worksheets independently. As a result of this assignment, I have found that my students develop a greater interest in the details of authors' lives and in the relation between authors' lives and work.

Jean Tittle, Gull Lake High School, Richland, Michigan

NOVEL IDEAS

My major goal for using novels in the teaching of reading is to promote lifelong reading habits in my middle school students by allowing for individual differences in student ability, by letting students choose their own activities, and by encouraging creative responses to reading.

These units are organized in a specific way. First, the students are given three sheets explaining the unit.

On the first sheet is a list of books (based on theme) and the directions. Note that the students have the option of finding appropriate books on their own.

Contract

Booklist

Island of the Blue Dolphins
Call It Courage
Julie of the Wolves
My Side of the Mountain

Hatchet
Other _____

Directions
1. Read any two of the books above.
2. Participate in your group discussions.
3. Choose one activity from List 1.
4. Choose one activity from List 2.

The time commitment is three weeks. Extra credit may be given for doing more than one activity from each list.

The second sheet contains the two activity lists.

List 1 (Writing Activities)
1. Write a short summary of the book.
2. Write a different ending of the book.
3. Choose a chapter, and write it in the form of a play.
4. Write a short story that could be a sequel to the book.
5. Write a poem based on the theme of the book.

List 2 (Art Activities)
1. Illustrate the setting and main characters of the book in a mural, diorama, or mobile.
2. Design a book jacket or poster to attract vendors to the book.
3. Portray the book's main characters using puppets, costumes, or portraits.
4. Paint a T-shirt to highlight significant characters, events, or themes in the book.
5. Plot the book's events on a game board.
6. Design an illustration that will enhance an important passage in the book.

On the third sheet are discussion questions that may apply to any book: questions about the author's writing style, about ideas gained from the book, about the characters—"Did they seem real?" "What were their most admirable traits?" Also, I often ask the students to read their favorite parts of the books. This sheet can be used in cooperative groups, and the discussion questions may be answered orally or in writing.

As part of an "integrated curriculum," I find this unit can be adapted in any number of ways. I also like the interactive learning involved, as student and teacher confer on a regular basis so that both know that the student is doing the work in an acceptable way before it is graded and points are awarded.

Mary A. Hummel, Fall Creek Middle School, Fall Creek, Wisconsin

VARIATIONS ON A THEME

As long as there are books, there will be book reports. But for many students, writing an interesting book report is a difficult assignment. After years of frustration, I've finally hit upon a technique that really works. I assign the reports to be written in letter form, from a vantage point other than that of a student.

In one version of this book-report assignment, the student is an agent for a publishing company. The student must now see the book not as a finished work, but as a manuscript submitted for consideration. The student as agent writes a comprehensive letter to the author telling the author if the book in question has potential. The agent must judge the strengths and weaknesses in the plot and characters, and must keep in mind audience appeal, readability, the author's style, and other factors. He or she gives the author advice as to what should be changed, and speculates about the author's potential for success.

In a second alternative to the standard book report, students assume the role of an editor of *Reader's Digest* condensed books and write to the author. To make this assignment more manageable, I require that the book read must be either an autobiography or a biography. Students write to tell the author that his or her book is to be included in the next condensed book by *Reader's Digest*, but that it must be shortened. Each student as editor describes in detail which portions of the book will be kept, which ones will be condensed, and which will be deleted. As editor, the student must be critical and thorough in describing what he or she thinks is most important in the story line.

In yet another possibility for a book report, students write a letter to me recommending that the book be required reading or that it be dropped from the reading list. They must cover the book's appeal to their peers, its literary merits, and, if applicable, the issue of censorship.

The possibilities for book reports in the form of letters are endless. By giving students an opportunity to assume a variety of voices, any one of these assignments should help them employ more creativity and experiment with various writing styles.

Judith A. Seaman, Hugoton High School, Hugoton, Kansas

BOOK REPORTS, NEW STYLE

I've been generally pleased with how ninth- and tenth-graders handle this supplementary reading assignment.

Directions: Read each of the following suggestions carefully. Select one and fully develop it in conjunction with the novel you have read.

1. You are the mother or father of a teenager, and you are writing to your sister or brother who also is the parent of a teenager. Either recommend the novel you read or explain why you think your

niece or nephew should not read the book. Use correct letter form. Cite specifics from the novel to support your point of view.

2. You are dining at a Chinese restaurant with the main characters from the novel you read. On that particular night the fortune cookies are amazingly appropriate. Tell what each fortune cookie said and why it was especially fitting to the character who received it. Don't forget to include yourself!

3. Write two or more consecutive entries in the diary of one of the characters.

4. Invite one of the characters in your book to dinner, explaining why you chose that character above the others. Next, write a note to your mother telling her that you have invited someone to dinner. Describe the person to her; include a few dos and don'ts for her to follow so that your guest will feel at home.

5. Lift a character out of the book and drop him or her down in our school. Is the character a student, teacher, custodian, secretary, nurse, principal, cafeteria employee, patron? Don't change the character's personality--just show what might happen if he or she became one of us!

6. Quote three passages from the book. Why did you select these above all others? Cite three or more specific reasons for each passage you select.

Edd W. Armstrong, North Salinas High School, Salinas, California

3 | EMPHASIS: THE NOVEL, MEDIA, AND THE ARTS

A CRITICAL LOOK AT NOVEL/MOVIE PAIRS

How many times have English teachers wished they had not assigned the research paper? Each is confident—before grading begins—that this year's crop will reveal true interest and marvelous discoveries. Wrong! Once again, the grading becomes laborious, the suspicions of plagiarism constant, the resolve to find another assignment for next year steadfast.

Years ago my students discovered the University of Houston's library to be the finest, most accessible source of pre-prepared research papers requiring a bit of money for the Xerox machines and a few hours at their computers for minor changes. They did not immediately realize that the style of writing would give them away. (Style—another opportunity for a lesson.)

I decided that I needed to produce an assignment that qualified as a research paper/critical analysis. Since Conrad's *Heart of Darkness* paired with Coppola's *Apocalypse Now* is a staple of my course, and because the students and I explore the parallels, changes, and effects produced from novel to movie, I determined to extend these lessons. I personalized an assignment allowing each student to become the critic and analyze his/her chosen novel and movie.

I compiled a list of approximately 140 titles of novels on which films have been based, making sure that the films were available through rental stores. In fact, I found the easiest way to compile the list was to browse through the "Classics" section of the local video stores. I and my students also added to the list by looking through the weekly TV listings for appropriate films scheduled to air on cable channels. I posted the list on the wall, instructing the students to choose any five titles and prioritize the list.

Our diverse list of novel/film pairs included works by Hemingway and Steinbeck, other commonly taught works such as *Catch-22* and *Lord of the Flies,* and still other works less often read in high school, such as Turgenyev's *Father and Sons*, Burgess's *Clockwork Orange*, and many others. Then I asked students to draw numbers to determine the order of selection so that first-period students did not have an advantage over sixth-period students. No two students read the same novel.

For several years this assignment culminated in a six- to ten-page essay discussing whether or not the director/producer was honest to the author's range of intentions. This year, however, I changed the reporting format and offered a number of options:

- an original six- to ten-page essay assignment
- an oral report presented as a book and movie review
- a written review such as those found in *The New Yorker*
- a billboard advertising the book and movie
- an art mode that captured the essence of novel and movie
- a videotape presentation
- a dramatic presentation of a scene or moment that had been altered from novel to movie
- a student suggestion approved by me

My directions for the project and criteria for grading were nonstifling and nontrivial. The students were expected to make clear to the audience the critical assessment of the director's treatment of the author's novel. The work should show:

- keen understanding of the original work and the subsequent movie
- original thought or observation
- creative presentation
- appropriate written or oral language skills

With the exception of the essay, each project was to be accompanied by a list of differences and a brief explanation of the impact of the alteration.

This year my twelfth-grade honors students revealed true interest and marvelous discoveries. They discovered their own potential for critical analysis, reviewing, writing, convincing, and presenting.

Marilyn L. Arehart, Alief-Hastings High School, Houston, Texas

PEARLS IN PAIRS

don't like to show the film versions of novels we are studying in my 10th grade American Literature classes. Instead, I prefer to show a film which parallels the novel in some ways and contrasts with it in others. Then, at the end of the unit of study, the students write papers which are nearly always interesting and insightful. Following are three combinations I have used with great success:

Cool Hand Luke (film)
One Flew over the Cuckoo's Nest (novel)

The Fighting 69th (film)
The Red Badge of Courage (novel)

Breaking Away (film)
The Great Gatsby (novel)

After the students have read the novel and viewed the film, I have them work in small groups on specific topics. Their task is to find and list all the similarities (and differences, if applicable) in that area. For example, some of the categories for the first pair, *Cool Hand Luke* and *One Flew over the Cuckoo's Nest*, might be:

Setting: The setting of each is an all-male institution (prison, mental institution) where the spirit and individuality of the men have been all but destroyed by those in charge.

Characters: The heroes are rebels who possess indomitable spirits, inspire the other inmates, become leaders and heroes to them, briefly give up their battles against the power structures, and perform one final, glorious achievement, knowing full well the consequences. Both are weakened by "recruits to their banners." Both are destroyed by the institutions, but their causes are taken up by their disciples.

Point of View: Comparable characters tell the story of the hero: the Chief tells the story of McMurphy and at the end of *Cool Hand Luke*, Dragline repeats Luke's story.

Imagery, Metaphor, Symbolism: Both use Christ imagery, animal imagery, and the motif of gambling. Both contain symbols for the lack of humanity of those in power--Boss Godfrey's glasses and the gun with which he "speaks" in *Cool Hand Luke*, and the Nurse's starched, tight uniform and "soldering iron" nail polish in *One Flew over the Cuckoo's Nest*.

Themes: Both emphasize the importance of community, commitment, integrity, humor, self-assertion, our need for heroes and for hope; both suggest that, as F. Scott Fitzgerald said, even if "things are hopeless [one must] live determined to see them otherwise."

The other two combinations work equally well. The very sentimental *Fighting 69th*, which supports unquestioningly the traditional view of military heroism as motivated by loyalty to God, country, and regiment, clearly illuminates the ironic tone of Crane's *Red Badge of Courage*, which expresses the Naturalist's skepticism regarding free will and morality. Both, however, describe the experience of a young man who goes to war for the first time hoping to become a hero, who runs away, and who eventually returns to fight heroically.

Breaking Away, like *The Great Gatsby*, addresses the American Dream, but unlike it, suggests that the Dream is still very much alive and well. Further, both of these works present the story of a young man from working class origins who seeks to better himself by creating a persona through which he almost, but not quite, wins the girl of his dreams.

We have great fun with these combinations in class, and they provide a wealth of material from which students can draw in writing their papers. Class discussion after each film helps students begin to consider the similarities and differences between the paired works. Then, when students' papers are completed, we have another open discussion in which students can compare the ideas and insights they came to while writing.

Linda S. Felice, Jesuit College Preparatory School, Dallas, Texas

MTV MEETS THE LITERATURE CLASSROOM

Do you and your students dread the old question-and-answer routine when studying a novel? Well, here's an innovative way to get off the road most traveled—appeal to one of the most important aspects of a teenager's life—music!

A middle school or high school student uninterested in music is rare, and after collecting more walkmans than my desk could hold, I decided to turn the tables on them. By appealing to students' interests and incorporating their favorite tunes with the novel they are reading, I devised a method that challenges the students and makes the project fun for the whole class.

First, I ask the students to form groups of two or three. I don't recommend using groups larger than this because of the amount of work and decision making involved.

The students collaborate in their groups to choose either a scene or character from the novel to interpret by using music.

After choosing a scene or character, the students then find a two-minute segment of the song that they feel best interprets the particular scene or character they choose. I recommend segments of no longer than two minutes for maximum effectiveness. The song might relate to the novel because of the lyrics or the overall mood the song emanates. I do not set parameters here either, because I want the students to be creative.

One student group, for example, chose the following song passage to illustrate the general mood of Chapter 2, "Castle Rock," in the novel *Lord of the Flies:*

"In the Name of the Father" by U2
(from the movie soundtrack)

I'll follow you down—
In the name of reason, in the name of hope,

In the name of freedom, you drifted away . . .
In the name of justice, in the name of fun . . .
In the name of the father, in the name of the son
Call to me . . .
No one is listening
I'm waiting to hear from you . . .

Another group chose lyrics to go along with Ralph's thoughts on being the sensible character after he is banished from the group of boys that Jack rules:

"Streets of Philadelphia" by Bruce Springsteen
(from the *Philadelphia* soundtrack)

I was bruised and battered, I couldn't tell what I felt
I was unrecognizable to myself
I saw my reflection in a window, I didn't know my own face
Oh brother are you gonna leave me wastin' away . . .

Finally, the students write a formal explanation of how they came to make their musical choices and how they relate to the scene or character in the novel.

The final aspect of this project is the presentation. The groups present their projects to the class by first playing the two-minute segment, and then explaining to the class their music choices as they relate to the novel. I allow approximately five minutes for each presentation.

This music project is not as easy an assignment as the students might perceive it to be. The students must be able to analyze and interpret the scene or character before they can find a song that relates to the novel. The students also must learn to work together in small groups to accomplish a task, and they must write a short essay. Finally, the students have an opportunity to practice their presentation skills.

I graded the projects on the following criteria: the originality of the music, the organization of the presentation, and the content of the essay.

This project works well with any novel. I often use this project when teaching *Lord of the Flies* by William Golding, and I am amazed to see how the music draws the students into the novel. Try to incorporate this fun project near the middle of the teaching of a novel when enthusiasm begins to wane. The students usually jump into this project, and with a sense of renewal, are ready to finish the novel. For some of my students, this project has meant the difference between liking and disliking the novel. In the MTV world that teenagers live in today, teachers cannot go wrong with this new approach to an old novel!

Melissa Smith, Pleasanton High School, Pleasanton, Texas

| VISUAL ESSAY

As my students studied *All Quiet on the Western Front* during the spring, they expressed considerable interest in the various themes and issues surrounding war. Some identified with the youthfulness of the soldiers in the novel, while others shared family stories from parents and grandparents who were veterans. Many became increasingly incensed with the inhumanity and injustice rampant in any such conflict. It became apparent that they were forming definite opinions about the nature and ethics of war itself. With Memorial Day approaching, I sought an expressive outlet for these attitudes and emotions. The result was a visual essay embraced by many of my students which made Memorial Day more than just one last holiday before the end of the school term.

The assignment was simple and straightforward: "Create a visual essay addressing the theme of war and peace to commemorate Memorial Day for staff and students at our high school." I defined a visual essay as a combination of visual images and carefully selected words used economically to express a personal feeling and/or viewpoint about a theme. Students could express a personal feeling and viewpoint about war, evoke an emotional and intellectual response in viewers, heighten viewers' awareness about the theme, and stimulate viewers to stop and think about war's effects and impact. Students could produce their visual essays individually or with one or two partners. Media could include video and music as well as more traditional formats such as drawings and photographs.

Specific guidelines that proved helpful in the students' work and my evaluation included these:

1. Express a *specific* viewpoint. "War is bad" is not specific.
2. Use words selectively and minimally. Think of a billboard where words need to be read quickly in passing.
3. Combine visual images and words to "pack a wallop" for the viewer.
4. Write the specific view that you are attempting to communicate on the back of your visual essay.

I suggested sources for words: quotations from actual veterans, war literature, song lyrics, war poems, *Bartlett's Familiar Quotations*, and original poetry. At least one student used each of these sources.

At the time the assignment was made, I spelled out the evaluation criteria: the specific message is clear to the viewer; the viewpoint is specific (not general); words are used economically; images and words work effectively in tandem; the visual essay makes the viewer stop and think about the theme; it has visual appeal/impact; sources of quotations are identified.

For publication we secured bulletin boards in the front hall of our school. The students selected which of the visual essays to display for the other students during the weeks before and after Memorial Day. A number of students produced videos for their projects, so the media center agreed to broadcast them over the in-house television system the day after Memorial Day. An announcement was placed in the school bulletin so that interested classes could tune in.

My students' response to this project was enthusiastic, creative, original, and in many cases moving. Two girls asked younger siblings and their friends to draw illustrations of their perceptions of war. Other students made a large flag quilt superimposed with clasped hands and the message, "Love is thicker than blood." Videos included one using images from a local national cemetery interspersed with death statistics from various wars to make its point. Another group of students collaborated with their parents who were Vietnam veterans to produce a video using memorabilia, images, and music from that era.

In a society where war is a media event and violence is becoming increasingly commonplace in the lives of young people, this project gave my students an opportunity to personalize the concept of war and explore its relationship to themselves. In so doing they discovered that they held strong, if not intense, feelings about this theme. Expressing their intensity in a creative outlet resulted in young people who had become more socially conscious, aware of their humanity, and able to articulate their views.

Patti Slagle, Seneca High School, Louisville, Kentucky

Willa Cather and Georgia O'Keeffe

EXPLORING THE TEXTS OF TWO AMERICAN ARTISTS

Buoyed by a doctoral course that explored the written works of Willa Cather (1873-1947) and the visual works of Georgia O'Keeffe (1887-1986), I decided to try to share with my students the bond between these two American artists, even though there is no evidence that they ever met or that they ever even made mention of one another. My intention was to expand this juxtaposition, but what follows here is a description of my first step—using O'Keeffe's paintings of the southwest landscape to *see* the landscape of Cather's *Death Comes for the Archbishop*. (This description focuses on a community college classroom, but the activity outlined would be accessible to many high school students.)

Cather's 1926 *Death Comes for the Archbishop* is certainly not the only Cather novel to deal with landscape or even the southwestern landscape; teachers interested in combining O'Keeffe and Cather might also consider Cather's *Song of the Lark* for another southwestern setting or *My Antonia* for a midwestern study of landscape.

My brief introduction to each artist included letting students share what they knew of Cather's and O'Keeffe's works and providing a few details from published biographies. (I was surprised to discover that, once I showed the class a photograph of O'Keeffe and a few reproductions of her work, including *Ram's Head with Hollyhock, Red and Orange Hills,* and *Red Canna,* many students recognized her work, having seen it on calendars, note cards, and T-shirts. As the semester went on, students took great pride in bringing to class little "O'Keeffe jewels," as they called them, found in bookstores and small galleries.)

Then, using color slides of photographs that I took myself, I was able to project O'Keeffe's canvas images against a blank, white classroom wall, and make them large enough to show detail and richness of color. Viewing the slides of O'Keeffe's vision of the southwest, while listening to a reading of Cather's written description of the same region, enhanced the students' appreciation both of the power of the brush and the power of the pen. The connections they made between the two artists' approaches and styles were sensitive and informed, as their responses (which I describe later) revealed.

What follows is a selection of the words of Cather that I chose to accompany the images of O'Keeffe. When I present this in class, I ask a guest reader, either another woman in our English department or a present or former student, to read Cather's words aloud as I operate the slide projector.

FROM DEATH COMES FOR THE ARCHBISHOP

The two priests rode side by side into Los Ranchos de Taos, a little town of yellow walls and winding streets and green orchards. The inhabitants were all gathered in the square before the church. (141)
Ranchos Church, oil on canvas, 1930, 24" x 35"

The cardinal had an eccentric preference for beginning his dinner at this time in the late afternoon, when the vehemence of the sun suggested motion. The light was full of action and had a peculiar quality of climax of splendid finish. It bored into the . . . trees, illuminating their mahogany trunks and blurring their dark foliage. (4)
Dead Trees with Pink Hill, oil on canvas, 1945, 30" x 4".

He must have traveled through thirty miles of these conical red hills, winding his way in the narrow cracks between them. They were so exactly alike one another that he seemed to be wandering in some geometrical nightmare . . . red as brick dust, and naked of vegetation except for small juniper trees. (17)

> *Stump in Red Hills,* oil on canvas, 1940, 30" x 24"
> *Cliffs Beyond Abiquiu,* oil on canvas, 1943, 30" x 16"
> *Red and Yellow Cliffs,* oil on canvas, 1940, 24" 36"

He was on a naked rock in the desert, in the stone age, a prey to homesickness for his own kind, his own epoch, for European man and his glorious history of desires and dreams. Through all the centuries that his own part of the world had been changing like the sky at daybreak, this people had been fixed, increasing neither in number nor desires, rock-turtles on their rock. (103)

> *The White Place in Shadow,* oil on canvas, 1942, 30" x 24"

Did you hear what happened to him at Abiquiu last year, in Passion Weeks? He tried to be like the Savior, and had himself crucified! Oh, not with nails. He had himself tied upon a cross with ropes, to hang there all night. They do that sometimes at Abiquiu, it is a very old-fashioned place. (154)

> *Black Cross,* New Mexico, oil on canvas, 1929, 39" x 30"
> *Grey Cross,* with Blue, oil on canvas, 1929, 36" x 24"

At the end of the slide presentation, I turned up the lights and asked the students to write for a few minutes in response to the images and words they had just seen and heard. Some students sat, quietly staring at the now bare, white wall where moments before O'Keeffe's reds and yellows and blacks had washed it. Others wrote quickly, filling the front of a page before I stopped them. Their responses were as varied as the students; one man in his twenties wrote that, as with music, art has the power to affect one physically: the blood pressure rises, and the heartbeat quickens. An older woman wrote that the story of the Archbishop was sadder to her now, now that she had seen his New Mexico. And finally, one student suggested I write to Viking, the publisher of the edition of *Death Comes for the Archbishop* we used, advising them to get permission to use *Ranchos Church* on future covers.

Was this venture into the humanities worth it for me? For the students? Did it give them another *reading* of Cather's text? Did it introduce them to an American artist, an unknowing soulmate to the writer? Did it invigorate me and revitalize my syllabus? It did all these things, and more. Because of my students' response to a humanities approach, I will continue it with

Walt Whitman and Thomas Eakins, and I will encourage my students to make connections across the arts so that their appreciation and joy in literature can transcend the printed page.

Anne Kuhta, Northern Virginia Community College, Manassas, Virginia

FINDING LESSONS IN SONG

This is a project I use with reluctant readers and writers in conjunction with the reading of Steinbeck's *The Pearl* (1947). Since my students are often struggling with low self-esteem, it is rewarding for them to be assigned a project that tests their creative ability rather than their mechanical ability.

While reading and discussing *The Pearl,* we focus on the importance of the moral or parable at the beginning of the story. I tell students that they have one week to pick out favorite songs or poems that they believe contain morals or good lessons that could apply to everyone's life. Of course, not all songs or poems communicate a moral, so a certain amount of discrimination is called for in choosing songs or poems. No two students can select the same song, to ensure a good variety. I ask students to check their choices with me before planning their presentations.

Each student is to play the song for the class or read the poem aloud, and to have a visual to go along with the poem or song. After explaining the visual, the student explains, in his or her own words, the moral or lesson to be derived from the song or poem.

In a class where it is ordinarily a struggle for students to stay on task and finish any given assignment, I was amazed at the results of this assignment. Students were excited and hardworking and beamed with a sense of pride at their own accomplishments. One girl presented the song "From a Distance," recently made popular by Bette Midler. We listened intently as the song played on the tape recorder. Afterward, she displayed a poster board to which she had attached war scenes clipped from magazines and yellow ribbons tied into bows. In the center of her poster she had placed a large photo of two small children hand in hand. As she talked about her song and explained that her uncle had been sent to the war in the Persian Gulf, tears rolled down her cheeks, and even the "tough" guys in the class were affected.

On a lighter note, another student chose the song "Every Rose Has Its Thorns" by the group Poison. Although this boy was a below-average student academically, he was an outstanding student artistically. His visual was a beautifully drawn rose surrounded by impressive sketches of well-known political, musical, and movie personalities. His analysis of the song was insightful; he explained that even a person who is rich and powerful has things about him or her that are not perfect.

There are obvious benefits to thinking and talking about the messages conveyed in songs and poems. In addition, this assignment shows insecure students that they, too, are capable of producing high-quality work in English class.

Cathy McKinney, Pendleton Heights High School, Pendleton, Indiana

AWAKENING STUDENTS WITH MUSIC

In discussions of Kate Chopin's novel *The Awakening,* students are eager to explore gender issues. Often, however, students polarize themselves along gender lines, boys siding with Léonce Pontellier and girls with

Edna. To encourage students to be sensitive to the complexities of Edna's awakening, we (two English teachers and a music teacher) collaborated on an interdisciplinary approach that would draw on students' love of music and their own struggle against conformity. This approach could be adapted for use with other literary works as well.

After listening to several preludes and impromptus by Frederic Chopin, we chose the "Fantasie in C# Minor" to play for students. This year we are including Isolde's song from "Tristan and Isolde," specifically mentioned in the text and described by Leonard Bernstein in *The Infinite Variety in Music* as an example of Romanticism.

When students finished reading Chapter 21, in which Edna is moved to tears by the music Mlle. Reisz plays, we introduced an activity that combines writing, drawing, and listening to music. First, we darkened the room, with only the word *awakening* on the overhead projector. One of the teachers then wrote on the overhead as students "clustered" around the word, calling out concrete phrases, images, and memories they associated with the word.

Next we passed out a large sheet of drawing paper and a box of crayons. We asked students to listen to the music and color the page, choosing crayons and drawing shapes that seemed appropriate for the feelings the music evoked. They could also write words if they wished. When the music ended, we asked students to write about a personal experience of awakening, a time when they felt jarred out of the norm. After about fifteen minutes, we asked for volunteers to read their responses. Clearly, the experience opened students to the impact of an emotional awakening and the impulse to defy the norm. As a result, students seemed more sensitive to Edna's feelings and the choices she makes.

On the following day, students who were also in music theory and appreciation classes examined the methods through which the composers evoked the responses from the listener. Thus these students had the actual experience of responding to the literature and an opportunity to analyze how the music drew forth their emotions. They were, as Aaron Copland describes in his introduction to *What to Listen for in Music*, active listeners. In retrospect, we would add this dimension for all students by asking their music teacher to meet with the literature students on the following day.

We also brainstormed other possibilities to enhance students' experiences. In the future we will incorporate some of the following strategies:

1. Show scenes from the movie *Impromptu* (Governor-Ariane/Hemdale, 1990) that illustrate the contrast between playing for a social occasion and playing for an audience that understands art. Then juxtapose "Moonlight Sonata" performed by Schroeder in the Broadway musical *You're a Good Man, Charlie Brown* and Arthur Rubinstein's sensitive rendering. These contrasts may help students understand Edna's response to Mlle. Reisz in Chapter 9. Students might discuss why Edna associates images with Adele's music but only feelings with Mlle. Reisz's music.

2. Ask students to bring in CDs or tapes of piano solos that have moved them, such as performances by George Winston, Billy Joel, or Elton John.

3. Discuss the effect of weaving Isolde's song from "Tristan and Isolde" with the "Fantasie Impromptu." Ask students to discuss this effect before writing about their experiences of awakening.

4. Play several types of background music while students read sections of the novel. Ask students to discuss how specific kinds of music affect their response to the written word.

5. Ask students to compile a bibliography of novels, short stories, films, and poems in which a person is awakened through music.

Katherine Hoffman, Beverly McColley, and Merle Becker, Norfolk Academy, Norfolk, Virginia

4 | EMPHASIS: THE NOVEL AND THE WORLD

WEBBING DICKENS

Imagine a class of seventh graders eagerly researching nineteenth-century England—and enjoying it!

What have I done to facilitate this? I introduced my students to the technique of *webbing,* also termed *semantic mapping.* (See *Writing the Natural Way* by Gabriele Lusser Rico, J. P. Tarcher, 1983, and *Use Both Sides of Your Brain* by Tony Buzan, E. P. Dutton, 1983.) Webbing is a graphic representation of main ideas and subpoints and the relationship between them. My students use this technique in researching Charles Dickens and his times, before reading *A Christmas Carol.*

First I asked students to research the question "What characteristics describe Dickens's world?" Not all webbing requires research, as it's sometimes useful to have students web what they already know about a topic, but in this case my options were to provide the necessary information in the form of a lecture or allow students to find it on their own. The librarian and I arranged on a corner table in the library all of the reference books that we thought students might use.

Before students began their research, we discussed in class what kinds of information they might want to know about nineteenth-century England. To help students brainstorm ideas, I asked them to picture the main sections of a newspaper and think of the kinds of news—politics, economics, business and labor, entertainment, art and literature, religion, and fashion trends. With those general topics in mind, we went to the library. For two days students read and took notes, acquiring a general picture of nineteenth-century England.

On day three I introduced webbing. With colored chalk I began a web with the central idea, "Characteristics of Dickens's World."

Students copied the central circle and the phrase inside. Next I asked students to suggest one of the major divisions that characterized nineteenth-century England. One student suggested "labor," and I wrote this on the chalkboard. Students suggested as subpoints "workhouses" and "debtors' prison," and I copied these onto the web as well. We then moved to the next main point, and as the web took shape, students began to see an overlap of ideas. With the addition of a few more topic headings, our partially completed web looked like this:

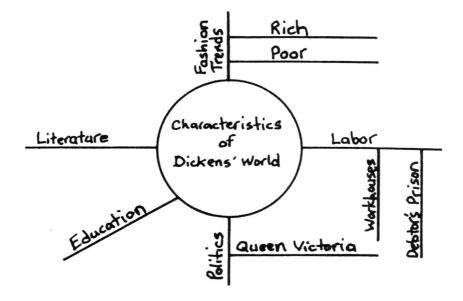

After we completed this web by adding subpoints to the remaining topics, I asked students to use some of the facts they learned in research to create webs of their own. I encouraged students to compare their completed webs and to discuss the different ways they found to organize the same facts.

The first year that I introduced webbing, I stopped when the web was complete and moved directly into the reading assignment, but I later saw other possibilities. For instance, as a prewriting activity, webbing could provide the basis for research reports, thus reducing the possibility of plagiarism.

Mary E. Purkey, Rudder Middle School, San Antonio, Texas

ETHICS QUESTIONNAIRE FOR STUDENTS

Before my junior English classes begin reading a novel, I often ask the students to complete what I call the ethics questionnaires. These short quizzes, which my students answer anonymously, pique their curiosity about the coming novel, provide a preview of the relevance of the literature to our society, and lay the foundation for excellent class discussions. I have been especially pleased with the use of these questions as a means of motivating students to begin difficult classic novels, which often seem unrelated to the lives they live.

Recently, before we began Hawthorne's *The Scarlet Letter*, I asked my juniors to answer ten "yes" or "no" questions about their views on sin, punishment, and guilt. My students were divided down the middle in answering the question, "Do you believe that physical pain should ever be part of punishment?" Not surprisingly, an overwhelming majority answered "yes" to the question "Have you ever done something wrong, not told about it, and suffered for your silence?"

SAMPLE ITEMS FROM PUNISHMENT QUESTIONNAIRE
(for use with The Scarlet Letter)

Answer *Yes* or *No* to the following questions:

1. Do you believe that physical pain should ever be part of punishment?
2. Should students who do not do their assignments be asked to stand in front of the class and recite this statement: "I did not do my assignment because this class and my grade are not important to me"?

3. Do you believe in expulsion from school as punishment for certain serious offenses?
4. If you were married and your spouse committed adultery, could you under certain conditions continue your marriage?
5. Have you ever done something wrong, not told about it, and suffered for your silence?

Last year, before we read Huxley's *Brave New World*, I asked my students to answer ten "agree" or "disagree" questions about where they believe our society is headed. Many of my students initially see the anti-utopian society portrayed by Huxley as nothing like twentieth-century America, and I wanted them to think about current trends that could perhaps head us toward Huxley's nightmarish creation. I asked them to agree (2 points), disagree (0 points), or remain undecided (1 point) with provocative statements such as "When I have even a slight headache or pain, I always take a pain reliever immediately." I told students that high scores might indicate some parallels between our society and Huxley's.

SAMPLE ITEMS FROM OUR SOCIETY QUESTIONNAIRE
(for use with Brave New World)

Give yourself 2 points if you agree with the statement, 1 point if you are undecided, and 0 points if you disagree.

1. I take a pain reliever such as aspirin at least once a month.
2. People who are chronically depressed should be given drugs to combat their depression.
3. Married couples who want children should be allowed to use test-tube fertilization.
4. I am a member of a particular political party because my parents belong to that party.
5. My parents would not like me to marry a person of another race.

After these questionnaires have been completed, I tabulate the class results and report them to the students. Sometimes I am shocked by their responses; often students are startled to realize that some of their answers are in the minority. Issues that seem clear-cut to students before we start often get a surprisingly mixed response, making students think and arousing their curiosity about the book we'll be reading. As we read the novels, then, I frequently refer to the questionnaires to reinforce the relevance of the literary themes to our lives. Students seem to remember these ethics questionnaires and our discussions about them. In fact, later in the year they often use these topics for research papers.

Judy Champney, Science Hill High School, Johnson City, Tennessee

LOOKING AT FREEDOMS IN LITERATURE

Applying the Bill of Rights to literature can provide a rich opportunity for open-ended discussions about themes, conflicts, setting, and characterization.

To use this approach, I first review with students the Bill of Rights and the freedoms described in the Amendments to the Constitution—freedoms *to* speech, press, peaceable assemblies, religion, due process, life, liberty, property, and trial by jury, and freedoms *from* cruel or unusual punishment, self-incrimination, unreasonable searches and seizures, and slavery or involuntary servitude except as punishment for a crime. I remind students that the Bill of Rights and Constitution are intended to offer equal protection for everyone and, when necessary, to protect individuals from the tyranny of the majority.

Then I focus attention on specific works of literature that students have read by asking students to suggest examples of rights to freedom, denials of freedom, and perceptions of freedom held by characters and by authors of these works. I also like to ask students to examine a particular work and to consider how the depicted freedoms and rights (or the lack of them) reflect the time period (i.e., the period during which a work was written and the period when the story's action was to have taken place), geographical location (i.e., the author's origin and where the story is set), and ethnic origins (the ethnic origins of the author as well as those of the story's characters). With a little experience, students are able to note parallels among the works they have read in terms of the freedoms and rights dealt with in each. This basic discussion is rekindled periodically throughout the year as a follow-up to reading assignments.

Obvious works to use with this approach are those with a historical base, such as Dickens's *Tale of Two Cities* or stories or writings about civil rights movements. But a great number of other literary works also offer discussion topics about the concepts set forth in the Bill of Rights. I pose questions to get students thinking, often using a "What if . . . ?" formula. Questions I pose over the course of a school year might include the following:

What if Tess in the "The Lottery" demanded due process? Would the social conditions inhibit that? If so, why'?

What if freedom of religion were allowed in the play *Becket?* How would the play be different?

If Shakespeare's *Richard III* had acknowledged freedom of speech, how would the drama be affected?

In Steinbeck's *The Pearl*, if the poor were not enslaved by ignorance and the tyranny of greed demonstrated by others, would Kino and Juana have experienced a different end to their pursuits?

Did Ethan Frome impose a type of slavery on himself as punishment for a crime that he perceived he committed? Was his action justified according to his social context?

How did the lack of equal protection and poor execution of due process influence the trial in *To Kill a Mockingbird?*

The discussions that grow out of these and similar questions are often serious and insightful. While deepening students' understanding of individual works of literature, these debates offer students a forum for considering their own rights and struggles for personal freedom and how these rights and freedoms might apply to other situations, times, and people.

Sheila Anne Webb, Cedar Rapids, Iowa

CONFRONTING THE LIMITS OF TECHNOLOGY

We've been contemplating our mechanical, electronic navels for too long.
—Ray Bradbury, "The Veldt," 1951

We Americans love technology. From personal computers to the latest electronic gadgetry for the kitchen, garage, or home entertainment center, we adults seem to have fallen in love with just about anything that will make our high-tech lifestyles more comfortable, convenient, and enjoyable. Our students are no different. They are fascinated by the latest developments in high-tech wizardry; they can talk endlessly about how they "must have" the newest CD player or video game and "can't live without" a Walkman or some rock star's music video. Yet, our students have embraced the benefits of a high-tech society without thinking about the possible negative effects of relying too much on technology.

Fortunately, students' interest in technology draws them to some of the excellent literature that explores the possible effects of technology on society. Ray Bradbury's often anthologized short story "The Veldt" (from his novel *The Illustrated Man*) speaks to the naive notions of youth concerning the potential dangers of technology. The story is Bradbury's frightening vision of the future in which a super-mechanized house first replaces the family and then destroys it. Students see the devastating results when parents allow machines to take over their roles as mother and father to their children. "The Veldt" suggests to students the dangers of believing in the unlimited potential of technology.

But there are other important reasons for studying this story. It allows students to examine their own views on technology and its place in society and to gain insight into the views of others. In addition, students begin to understand that there may be limits to what technology can do.

This story might also serve as an introduction to more complex works of literature by Bradbury or other authors that examine issues related to science and technology and their possible effects on society. For example, students might read Bradbury's *Fahrenheit 451* (1953), *The Martian Chronicles* (1950), or *The Illustrated Man*, George Orwell's *1984* (1949), Aldous Huxley's *Brave New World* (1932), or E. M. Forster's "The Machine Stops" (1928). In addition, while science fiction is a mainstay of adolescent literature, most students have not studied this literature that so many of them enjoy. Therefore, another important reason to have students read "The Veldt" is that it provides an opportunity for them to examine closely a key element of this fiction, as well as of literature in general—irony.

EXPLORING STUDENT OPTIONS

I begin with an activity that utilizes students' ideas and opinions about technology and family life. Before students read the story, I ask them to fill out a handout sheet entitled "Technology and Family Life Opinionnaire." (See page 88.)

After students have responded to all the statements on the opinionnaire, I compile the results on the board. Then, beginning with the statements for which there is the most disagreement, I lead a class discussion that focuses on students' responses to each statement. I encourage students to explain the reasoning behind their responses and to debate differing opinions. Since the statements on the opinionnaire require students to take a stand, a lively discussion invariably ensues.

One purpose of the opinionnaire and the follow-up discussion is to create interest in the characters and issues in the story students are about to read. Items No. 3 and No. 14, for example, relate to one aspect of the problem faced by the parents in the story. The family in the story, the Hadleys, own a "Happylife Home" equipped with all of the latest electronic machinery. The parents, however, have become concerned about the playroom, or nursery, where whatever thoughts or fantasies their ten-year-old children have are instantly reproduced in three dimensions, including the physical sensations one would associate with the fantasies. The Hadley children have been spending a lot of time creating a frightening fantasy about the African Veldt. Their fantasy is destructive and deadly: Lions kill and eat what seems to the parents to be an animal, and vultures feast on the remains. The Hadleys have exercised no control over the children's use of the playroom. They have started to feel useless and can see that they have allowed the playroom take their place as parents. When they try to turn the playroom off, they discover too late that it has already taken their place—it is alive—and they are the meal that the lions and vultures are feeding on in their children's fantasy.

Students' responses to the items on the prereading opinionnaire usually indicate that many of them believe that children should have more control over what they watch on television, and they either dismiss the idea that parents use television as a babysitter or claim that it does no harm. Bradbury suggests that parents should exercise considerable control over what children are permitted to watch on television, particularly when it comes to violence. He also indicates that parents who use television as a babysitter run the risk of destroying the family. Through the class discussion of the opinionnaire, students begin to question some of their initial responses and are motivated to find out how characters will deal with these issues in the story.

Another purpose of the opinionnaire is to provide a framework or context that will help students overcome their initial difficulty with the seemingly alien world they are confronted with when they start reading "The Veldt." However, through discussion of the items on the opinionnaire, students realize that the story's supermechanized house, playroom, and "odorophonics" are simply extensions of the kinds of electronic gadgetry available today.

The framework that the opinionnaire provides also helps students understand what the author of the story wants readers to understand about the potential dangers of technology. Many students have an oversimplified view of technology. They readily accept the notion, as stated in statement No. 1, that technological advances make life better for everyone. In discussion of the opinionnaire, students are often surprised to discover that some of their classmates do not share their optimism regarding technology. Some students point to pollution or to problems with nuclear power plants or to other technology-related disasters as examples of the potential drawbacks of technological advances.

In addition, in discussing statements No. 1 and No. 13, for example, students are encouraged to consider a wide range of possible ideas related to technology. As we discuss the various ideas that students bring up, they begin to consider the ways that technology has impact on their lives. These questions and others on the opinionnaire help students construct a framework or cognitive map that will better enable them to understand the story they are about to read.

Once we have discussed most or all of the statements on the

opinionnaire, I ask students to read the story. Then I lead a brief class discussion of the story, making sure students have a basic understanding of the plot and the sometimes tricky technical details that can really test their "willing suspension of disbelief." For example, I make sure that they understand the various services performed by the Hadleys' "Happylife Home" and can define words like "odorophonics" in terms of the story.

THE AUTHOR'S MESSAGE AND STUDENTS' LIVES

Once I am sure students have a basic understanding of the story and important technical details, they are prepared to deal with the irony in how the author is telling us about technology. I divide the class into small groups and ask them to determine from evidence in the story how Bradbury would probably respond to the fourteen statements on the opinionnaire. In addition, I ask students to respond to this question: Lydia Hadley says that the playroom is supposed to help their children work off their neuroses in a healthful way, but if this is true, how do you explain what happens in the end? In other words, what is Bradbury saying about technology?

After working out responses to these questions, the class reassembles to discuss and debate their findings. As the groups report their answers, students begin to formulate important conclusions. They realize, for example, that instead of helping the children, the playroom "becomes," as the psychologist in the story says, "a channel toward—destructive thoughts." Students also realize that it is the parents who are responsible. The Hadleys spoil their children and place all of their faith in technology. They allow the playroom to replace them as parents; ironically, the technology that replaces them as parents finally kills them. In addition, students realize that Bradbury echoes the comment Albert Einstein made about technology in a speech at the California Institute of Technology in February 1931: "Why does this magnificent applied science which saves work and makes life easier bring us so little happiness? The simple answer runs: Because we have not yet learned to make sensible use of it."

Discussing the fourteen statements on the opinionnaire in terms of what Bradbury would probably say about them is an important element in helping students interpret the irony and formulate conclusions about the story. For example, it is through this discussion that many students come to see that while George and Lydia Hadley might agree that "Technological advances make life better for everyone" (statement No. 1), Bradbury would probably not agree. In fact, Bradbury is suggesting exactly the opposite.

This discussion also helps guide students toward a reevaluation of their own views about technology. In considering what Bradbury would say about the statements on the opinionnaire, students inevitably end up comparing their responses to the statements before they read the story against their observations about the story. Often opinions have changed. In the middle of explaining how Bradbury would have responded to statement No. 5, one student suddenly blurted out, "You know, yesterday I was all for giving even little kids more freedom in deciding for themselves what and when to watch TV. But now, I think parents should set strict limits." Students begin to see the impact that the story has had on them.

FOLLOW-UP ACTIVITIES

In discussing which statements on the opinionnaire Bradbury would probably agree or disagree with and why, there is usually considerable disagreement about some. This disagreement provides a natural follow-up writing situation. I ask students to write a composition explaining why they think Bradbury would agree or disagree with one of the statements the class is having a problem with. I encourage each student to write it in the form of a letter to one of the others in the class who disagrees with his or her viewpoint.

Another possible follow-up activity is to have students read on their own another story that involves technological advances and their possible effects and that uses irony to convey its meaning. Then I have students write an interpretation of the story. I use either Gordon R. Dickson's "Computer's Don't Argue," from *You and Science Fiction* (National Textbook Company, 1979), or Isaac Asimov's "The Fun They Had," from *Impact: Fifty Short Short Stories* (Harcourt Brace Jovanovich, 1986). These follow-up activities reinforce skills students have developed in reading and analyzing "The Veldt"; they also serve as a means to determine their mastery of those skills.

Larry R. Johannessen, Saint Xavier College, Chicago, Illinois

Technology and Family Life Opinionnaire

Directions: Read each of the following statements. Write *A* if you agree with the statement or *D* if you disagree with it.

Agree or
Disagree

_____ 1. Technological advances make life better for everyone.

_____ 2. Most parents spend too little time with their children.

_____ 3. Parents should exercise more control over what their children watch on TV.

_____ 4. If people let machines do too much for them, then eventually people will no longer be able to do things for themselves.

_____ 5. Children should be given more freedom in deciding what to watch and when to watch TV.

_____ 6. Most teenagers do not try to spend time or talk with their parents.

_____ 7. It is dangerous to place too much faith in technology.

_____ 8. Most parents try to talk with their kids about problems.

_____ 9. It is possible to become addicted to television viewing.

_____ 10. Teenagers try to talk with their parents, but most parents never really seem to listen.

_____ 11. Most teenagers watch too much television.

_____ 12. Children who watch too much television often believe that the violent shows they watch portray life as it actually is.

_____ 13. Those who worry about the negative effects of technology should think about the many modern conveniences available today.

_____ 14. Parents too often use TV as a kind of babysitter for their children.

USING *FAHRENHEIT 451* TO DEBATE CENSORSHIP

Several years ago I heard Ray Bradbury tell a spellbound audience of high school students how he wrote his first novel, *Fahrenheit 451*, on a coin-operated typewriter in a library basement. Afterwards, I reread several of his works and decided to teach *Fahrenheit 451*, concentrating on the theme of censorship, to a class of junior students with low to average ability.

While students were reading the first of the novel's three sections, I focused classroom discussion on language usage and the structure of the novel, including plot, characterization, and setting. The low reading level and simple plot structure in contrast with extensive use of figurative language techniques in the narrative make *Fahrenheit 451* an ideal vehicle to teach or review metaphor, simile, and allusion.

When students were ready to move on to Parts Two and Three, I shifted our focus to Bradbury's theme of censorship versus the freedom to read. Our analysis began with list making. Students used their books to find all the different types of media which Bradbury mentions being censored. (More recently, students called my attention to a type Bradbury missed: music video censorship.) Students agreed that in *Fahrenheit 451* most of our common forms of communication are illegal except under strict supervision and in digest form.

Next, students reviewed the text for Bradbury's opinion of censorship. They found helpful the conversation between Montag and Beatty, in which Beatty tells the history of censorship (pp. 57–67 in the 1979 Ballantine edition), as well as Faber's analysis of conditions leading to his lost job as English teacher (pp. 96–97). As students stated Beatty's reasons for censorship, I listed them on the chalkboard:

cut long books to summaries because people had no time to read
  books
cut courses like English and history out of curriculum
close theaters
use more pictures and cartoons
omit anything objectionable to minorities
censor any controversial or thought-provoking ideas

To this list students added other reasons for censorship. They mentioned that Bradbury's world does not censor pornography and ours does. I defined the phrase *without redeeming social value* and the words *slander* and *libel* before adding them to our list.

Through anecdote and questioning, I called students' attention to the differences between total and partial censorship. I pointed out that parts of a book may be taken out as unsuitable, or a book or magazine may be called unsuitable for readers under a certain age. Other books are censored by being unobtainable in certain parts of the country. I explained that because of unflattering descriptions, *Grapes of Wrath* was not in the local library collection when I was growing up in Oklahoma. More recently Waukegan, Illinois, schools took *Huckleberry Finn* off the shelves after local protests. As part of our discussion, we considered Bradbury's comment that no writer can please every segment of an audience.

The class concluded their investigation of censorship by examining Bradbury's own words. Our edition of *Fahrenheit 451* contains an afterword in which Bradbury tells of censorship of his own work. Ironically, editors of this edition cut seventy-five bits and pieces from editions of *Fahrenheit 451* in the years since its first publication in 1953. Students were amazed to discover that the innocent language of the novel that they read had been subjected to censorship in earlier versions. Reading the afterword gave students the author's view of the sanctity of his writing. As Bradbury concludes, "I will not go gently onto a shelf, degutted, to become a non-book" (p. 184).

By this time the class was ready to attack the problem of censorship from a different perspective. I assigned the students the problem of responding to censorship of a novel. Students were allowed to choose *Fahrenheit 451* or a novel read earlier in the semester. The assignment was to write a letter to the novel's author or publisher or to a newspaper in reply to supposed censorship. Students could argue for or against censoring all or parts of a book or could explain why the book in question should not be censored. I gave each student a copy of the instructions below, a list of novels to choose from, and a summary of topics in those novels that might be likely to come under fire. I also supplied students with a review of censorship problems in *Huckleberry Finn* as a sample of the type of writing they were to produce. A useful resource at this point was *Celebrating Censored Books* (Wisconsin Council of Teachers of English, 1985), which gives examples of replies to censorship.

CENSORSHIP WRITING ASSIGNMENT

1.   Working with a partner, choose one of these books that you both have read. You will each need to find a copy of the chosen book to use as a reference.

     The Contender   *To Kill a Mockingbird*
     The Outsiders   *Of Mice and Men*
     A Separate Peace   *Durango Street*
     Lord of the Flies   *Fahrenheit 451*
     West Side Story

2.   Working together, make a list of all the reasons your book could be censored. Next to each reason describe or quote the exact part of the book which is censorable for that reason. These reasons for censorship could include language, racism, prejudice of some other sort, violence, criticism of government, criticism of religion, sex, use of drugs, suicide, and antipatriotic or antiwar messages.

3.   Write a letter to the book's author or publisher or to a newspaper explaining why this book should or should not be censored. You may choose to defend the book or to censor it. Your position does not necessarily have to be one you agree with. In writing your letter, use the reasons from your list.

     If you are writing in support of censorship, explain what ideas or elements are offensive and tell why. Use specific examples from the book. Also explain why it would be harmful for others to read the book.

     If you are writing in an effort to abolish (get rid of) censorship, explain what issues others have found offensive and give their reasons. Then explain why you feel the book should not be censored. Give reasons why other people should read the book.

     Your letter should be about two pages in length. It should

be well written, properly addressed, and neatly completed. You must turn in all your work, including your list, notes, first draft, and final copy.

I assigned the writing of a first draft for homework. In class the next day, pairs of students met again and exchanged papers to read and edit. Students spent two days on prewriting and fifteen to thirty minutes on editing.

Writing about a specific example of censorship fulfills several objectives. Bradbury's novel acquires relevance as students see censorship as an element in their lives. This open-ended assignment allows students latitude in the use of style and tone. Better writers use satire effectively in protesting against a novel; and less able writers feel secure in using a familiar novel in order to discuss censorship. Students practice the real-life skills of examining an issue and organizing a paper presenting the evidence from a specific viewpoint.

I have repeated this exercise several times, and each time am pleasantly surprised at how well students succeed with their papers.

Jill Martin, Warren Township High School, Lake Forest, Illinois

LETTERS FOR AND AGAINST *HUCKLEBERRY FINN*

In teaching *Huckleberry Finn* recently, I mentioned to my students the contradictory ways in which this novel is regarded. On the one hand, it is often attacked by censors who demand that it be removed from the high school curriculum, yet it is also widely considered the one classic of American literature that every high school student should read. My students were fascinated by this contradiction; we spent the rest of the class discussing the arguments for and against *Huckleberry Finn,* censorship in general, and the movie rating system.

When it came time to draw up the semester exam, I decided to return to the issue of censorship. I told my students that hypothetical "Westphalia" high school had decided to ban the book from the junior reading list, and asked them to write letters to the school administration stating their views in the matter. I asked that they respond politely, either refuting or supporting the administration's arguments based on their own understanding of the book.

Students put a lot of thought into their arguments, and their letters showed it. Here is one excerpt from a letter written for this assignment:

> Mr. Twain wrote "Huckleberry Finn" in order to show the people of America how they act towards one another. . . . These characters, who represented our society, were satirical characters used by the author. Just as Jonathan Swift did in "Gulliver's Travels" or as a cartoonist does daily, Mr. Twain was making a political statement about the moral condition of our country. He felt people should be kind and friendly to each other, no matter what race they are . . . .
>
> The final accusation of encouraging kids to go off on their own from society again was misinterpreted. Here, too, Twain was just

showing people that society's values were mixed up, and it took a child and a run-away slave to show what their values really should have been.

I believe this assignment worked because it gave students a format that they were comfortable with and a clear purpose and audience for their writing. It also allowed them to demonstrate their understanding of the novel. Equally important, it gave students a forum to respond in an adult way to those who decide what students will or will not be allowed to read.

Mark Cummings, Block Yeshiva High School, St. Louis, Missouri

A NOVEL BOOK REPORT IDEA

After having read, discussed, and written in response to several novels, each of my students picks a novel to be the subject of an individual oral book review. The choice of the novel is up to the student, but I explain that part of the book review will be a discussion or explanation of a related topic, which will require some research. Then I distribute lists of possible novels and topics, which I go over briefly so that students will have an idea of how the contents suggest related topics.

Some of the combinations that have been successful are listed below. (Check to be sure that these books have been included in your curriculum guide.)

Plague Dogs—using animals in research
Fahrenheit 451—censorship
Coma—organ transplants
I Am the Cheese—the FBI and the Government Witness Protection Plan

The Terminal Man—brain research, neurosurgery, epilepsy
The Invisible Man—racism
Alas, Babylon—nuclear war
I Never Promised You a Rose Garden—mental illness
Sticks and Stones—homosexuality
Brave New World—in vitro fertilization
Elmer Gantry—bogus evangelists
Of Mice and Men—retardation
A Tree Grows in Brooklyn—immigration
The Chocolate War—peer pressure
A Death in the Family—death
A Teacup Full of Roses—drugs
Player Piano—the dehumanizing effects of technology
Ordinary People—suicide
Going After Cacciato—Vietnam and the horrors of war

After students read through the titles and topics on this list, encourage them to choose their own books and topics if they like, subject to your approval.

Before students begin work, I explain that the oral presentation should last from nine to twelve minutes. I suggest that students spend two to four minutes focusing on the book, one to three minutes talking about the author, and five to eight minutes discussing the research topic. I suggest that the book review segment include mention of the author's style and the development of setting, character, and plot. I advise students to use aspects of the plot to illustrate their points but to give no more than a very brief summary of the story line. (It's a good idea to remind students periodically during the preparation period to tie their talk to the book as much as possible.)

I schedule several library days, during which students can do the necessary research for their reports. To add interest to the presentations, I require visual or audio aids. I read the following list of possibilities aloud to provide inspiration: pictures (gathered or created), charts, maps, graphs, readings, original book jackets or movie posters, appropriate personal slides (one of my students raised others' consciousness with slides of his retarded brother), a collage depicting theme or characterization, results of informal polls, a dramatic interpretation, a creative use of the audience (one student demonstrated the experience of discrimination by passing out red and green stickers and then discriminating against those holding the reds), costumes, staged events (a protest march), relevant songs or writings (Burns's "To a Mouse" for *Of Mice and Men*, Seeger's "Little Boxes" for *Babbit*), etc.

I schedule four reports a day and give each student a set day on which to be ready. When grading, I use peer evaluations and individual evaluations, as well as my own evaluation. I grade according to content, organization, creativity, presentation, audience appeal, the student's evaluation of time spent and work required, my observation of the same during class time, and information provided.

My informal observation of the results of this project is that the preparation and the presentation of these talks stimulate interest not only in specific books but in the related topics as well.

Jill VanAntwerp, Lowell Senior High School, Lowell, Michigan

5 | EMPHASIS: BRITISH NOVELS

A TALE OF
TWO CITIES

Have you considered dusting off the class set of *A Tale of Two Cities* this semester? It's a novel that many of us have neglected. True, there are problems with the assignment: Dickens's Victorian language and manners, his failure to go straight to the heart of the matter, his tendency to ramble (despite the short chapters), his habit of picking up one plot and set of characters only to put them down at an exciting moment to move to another plot and set of characters. Today's students protest these techniques. Some regard them as time-wasting, and a few consider them downright dishonest. Yet the story, as it has done so often in the past, will lure students into reading on; when they have finished, they will feel elevated by the experience.

To coax students past the initial hurdles of language, you might consider showing the film version first. Students will understand how the novel itself fills out and enriches the film's structure. Or, you may wish to delay the film until the study of the novel is complete, which preserves the imaginative element so vital to the reading experience. Either way, viewing the film serves to pull the plot together.

Here are some ways to work with this famous classic. Adapt the ones that fit your students and your purposes, and add favorites of your own.

SMALL GROUP ACTIVITIES

1. Divide the class into six groups and assign the following tasks. More than one group may be assigned the same task.

   a. Diagram the main plot and its subplots. Present your work as a poster or in a discussion at the chalkboard.
   b. List examples of Dickens's use of darkness and light, of numbers, and of colors (red and black). Be prepared to comment on what you have found.

  c. Find several examples of each of these figures of speech: hyperbole, metaphor, personification. Share your findings with the class along with an assessment of the effectiveness of those figures of speech.

  d. Collect passages that illustrate attitudes and values of the aristocracy and of the peasants. Draw conclusions to share with the class.

  e. Examine the beginnings and the endings of the chapters, books, and novel. What insights do you gain?

  f. Compare the novel's opening paragraph with the passage in Ecclesiastes, "To everything there is a season." Be prepared to comment on the use and effectiveness of the balanced sentences. How does the opening paragraph set the stage for the novel's many paradoxes?

2. Appoint an editorial board that will portion out responsibilities for creating a newspaper based on a single day in the novel—perhaps the day of Sidney Carton's execution. All types of newspaper writing should be included: news, human interest stories, editorials, classified and commercial ads, advice column, sports, cartoons, stock market and business reports, society pages.

3. Encourage the history buffs with this assignment. Divide the class into small groups and ask each group to choose a period in history, including today's history-in-the-making. Then ask each group to use chapter one, "The Period," as a model to show in writing or in an oral presentation how the period they chose represents both "the best of times and the worst of times."

4. An alternate assignment for history buffs is to read parts of Thomas Carlyle's *The French Revolution* (Dickens's source for factual information) and other writings about this uprising and to compare them with Dickens's fictional version.

5. Future thespians will enjoy forming small groups to write and then enact or read aloud a new final chapter for the novel. In it, Charles Darnay will be executed and Lucie will return home, later marrying Sidney Carton. What will happen to the doctor as a result of his failure to save Charles's life? Will Sidney change and lead a life free from the evils of alcohol and sloth? Don't be surprised if this assignment produces a modern soap opera!

DISCUSSION QUESTIONS

1. What statement about revolution does the book make?
2. Can the story be read as an allegory? For starters, what might the two cities represent?—The Republic and the Guillotine? Echoing footsteps and hundreds of people? Lucie and Madame DeFarge? In how many ways and by how many people is the phrase "recalled to life" applied?
3. List paradoxes found in the novel. What does Dickens's reliance on paradox suggest? Consider examples of evil resulting from good (the Revolution) and good coming from evil (the "hero"—if that is Darnay—is not so much the hero as is Carton, the "bad guy").
4. Discuss how women are portrayed: Lucie, Madame DeFarge, Miss Pross, Mrs. Cruncher, The Vengeance, the little seamstress, and the women of the Revolution. Then turn to the men: Lorry, Darnay, Carton, Cruncher, the Monsignor, Monsieur DeFarge, the various Jacques. Draw conclusions.
5. What statement does the novel make about taking risks? Which characters take risks and why? Who succeeds and who fails? Does what you discover help you to define what "success" and "failure" mean?

WRITING ASSIGNMENTS

1. Write an essay discussing how Dickens's style reflects his interest and involvement in journalism and in acting.
2. Choose one of the following quotations and write an essay that illustrates how the quotation is reflected in the novel.

   a. "The treasures of the rich are bought with the tears of the poor." (Thomas Fuller, 1732)
   b. "The Revolution is like Saturn—it eats its own children." (George Büchner, 19th century)

3. Investigate one of the following topics. Then write an informative essay comparing the subject as Dickens presents it with the same subject as you find it today: banking, prisons, revolutions, role of women, class lines. As an alternative, investigate the term *Jacques* as it was used in the French Revolution. Go on to find out how underground activities in various countries (Nazi Germany,

Poland) at various times compare with those of France.

4. You are Dr. Manette. Write a journal entry dated on the first night of your imprisonment.

5. Write an analysis of Darnay's two trials identifying what changed and why. Include details about the fickle masses.

6. Select one of the following pairs of characters and write a comparison/contrast essay: Carton and Stryver, Carton and Darnay, Miss Pross and Madame DeFarge, Lucie and Madame DeFarge.

Beverly Haley, The Language Works, Fort Morgan, Colorado

Dickens and Historical Perspective
A TALE OF TWO CITIES

The place of Dickens in high school British Literature courses seems secure. The question is not so much *whether* to read Dickens, as it is *which* of his works to read. Many opt for *Great Expectations*, perhaps because it is the most tightly written of his novels. An older favorite, though less structured and lapsing sometimes into Victorian sentimentality, may deserve another look. *A Tale of Two Cities*, with its historical panorama and detailed verbal picturization, can be a very effective tool for drawing a class not only into Dickens's art but also into the political conflicts of his era.

"It was the best of times, it was the worst of times." The profound ambiguity that Dickens felt towards both the historical events and his characters in this novel is apparent from its opening words. The evils of the *ancien régime* are detailed in such episodes as the death of the little girl under the speeding wheels of the Marquis's coach. The excesses of the Republic are as apparent not only in the butchery of the prisoners but also in the guillotining of the little seamstress who is as much an innocent victim as the girl.

Their criminal insensitivity to the plight of the impoverished cannot deprive the imprisoned aristocrats of dignity as they face their impending doom with restraint and evening entertainments. Nor can the justice of her cause excuse Madame Defarge's insistence that not only Charles Darnay but also Lucie and her daughter must die as well. Both social classes share the same flaw in Dickens's eyes. "The two regimes of France—the old order of the Marquis St. Evremonde and the new of the revolutionary Defarges—exalt their class, their abstract principles, above . . . personal ethics" (Angus Wilson, *The World of Charles Dickens*, New York: The Viking Press, 1970, p. 262). Perhaps by studying briefly those abstract principles, students can see and appreciate more clearly the fatal blindness that afflicts almost all of Dickens's characters in this novel.

First Phase: Background

To prepare the students for reading the novel intelligently, a great deal of background is necessary. Students with different interests and abilities can volunteer for or be assigned to appropriate prereading projects designed to provide a schema for understanding the novel. They can readily investigate certain key historical elements and prepare posters and handouts for in-class presentations. A timeline charting the key events of 1770 to 1790 is helpful, as is a chart of the titles and hierarchy of the British and French nobilities and of the structure of each government. A graph showing the distribution of wealth within the population, perhaps contrasted with a similar one for contemporary America, would reveal the differences between the diverse societies. A model guillotine helps too, as would a model of the Bastille.

As the final stage of preparation, the students should receive the *Declaration on the Rights of Man and of the Citizen* adopted by the French National Assembly on August 29, 1789 (available from the *Encyclopedia Britannica*). Subsequent class discussion can focus on the contrast between this declaration and the American Declaration of Independence. Especially effective is paralleling on the chalkboard the rights detailed by the American Bill of Rights and the French Declaration.

Second Phase: Reading the Novel

Because of the length of the work, three visual techniques can help keep student interest up.

First, a map of the territory between London and Paris can be prepared as a useful graphic organizer. Moving markers of different shapes or colors can provide a sense of location for each character as the action shifts from place to place.

Second, organizing a list of "doubles" on the board (cities, trials, mobs, and so on) and adding to it section by section as the book is read can sensitize students to Dickens's underlying structure.

Third, organizing lists of parallel images in the same way can sensitize students to that element in Dickens's art. The color red, sounds, roads--these are three easily recognized and very important recurring images.

Third Phase: Reactions

The first strategy for generating student writing about the novel would be to use the lists of doubles and images to explore concrete themes in an organized way. This approach would give students an excellent chance to practice simple writing. Or, a more imaginative approach would be student narratives in which students placed themselves at the foot of the guillotine, for example.

A second strategy would be to compare and contrast this novel with others dealing with the same or similar historical events and attitudes. *The Scarlet Pimpernel* comes immediately to mind, though some revolutionary novels of the twentieth century might also be appropriate. Possibilities might include Chinua Achebe's *Things Fall Apart*, Maya Angelou's *I Know Why the Caged Bird Sings*, Ernest Hemingway's *For Whom the Bell Tolls*, John Steinbeck's *The Grapes of Wrath*, and Richard Wright's *Native Son*. Video cassettes of film adaptations of some of these novels are available.

Students can delve further into historical evaluation or critical thinking through a third technique for generating student reaction, based on Dickens's depiction of women in the novel. Dickens is ambiguous about the events and the characters in this novel because he knew from his reading of history that both French regimes had been blind to their own failings. From the perspective of contemporary issues, the same charge could be leveled against Dickens himself. His women characters are dominated by men. The only exception is Madame Defarge, whose liberation has created a monster.

The students may receive a copy of the Seneca Falls Declaration of Sentiments and Resolutions on Woman's Rights of July 19, 1848. (Available in H. S. Commager's *Documents of American History*, Appleton, Century, Crofts, 1973.) When contrasted with the previous documents, this declaration reveals one point very clearly. The rights being claimed are no longer merely political and economic but profoundly personal: education, moral independence, and self-fulfillment. From a contemporary viewpoint, the document is an amazing foreshadowing of much of the feminist movement. (An important historical footnote is that one third of the signers of this declaration were men.)

Students could explore Dickens's presuppositions about the role of women in society. Which women does he seem to admire? Which women appeal to us today? Have standards for men changed in a similar way?

Interested students could also research the British or American suffragettes and contrast these women with those in this novel. Which kind of woman came to dominate the later struggle for women's rights?

The same lesson of the moral ambiguity of all revolutions could be pursued into other areas of literature. Works dealing with racism, sexual liberation, and so on are widely available. Without proselytizing, we can help our students become more aware of the great conflicts that face our century, just as Dickens dealt with those of his age.

> *A Tale of Two Cities* is a profoundly thoughtful, if not a theoretical book. It is the sort of novel that should be enormously usable for young people and their teachers . . . . Its conception can vivify for us the meanings of the past, can offer us a reading of history, humane and deep, by a great artistic intelligence. (G. Robert Strange, "Dickens and the Fiery Past," *20th Century Interpretations of A Tale of Two Cities*, Prentice-Hall, 1972, p. 75.)

Michael Marchal and John Hussong, Saint Zavier High School, Cincinnati, Ohio

HARD TIMES

Why choose *Hard Times* by Charles Dickens for class study? Foremost among the reasons, the novel helps young readers discover that relationships between adults and young people of another time have likenesses to, as well as differences from, such relationships today. Students also identify with the problems of Louisa and Tom Gradgrind in their efforts to become independent adults. In Dickens's satire of the ills of society, students see the beginnings of concern over the environmental, social, and personal effects of industrialization; such observations are particularly interesting at a time when we are witnessing what may, in the final analysis, prove to be the death of industrialization. Finally, *Hard Times* provides an opportunity to acquaint students with the work of an author who is widely acclaimed. This particular book, his most "single-minded social novel," can be read in a unit along with other books of social criticism and will stimulate discussions about character and caricature.

CLASS DISCUSSION

Although teachers have their own favorite questions for introducing and analyzing the novel, here are a few that I regularly use.

1. Discuss the title. In what ways can the word *hard* be used? The word *times*? How are we—as a group, as a nation, as individuals—having hard times today? What's different about our hard times and those of Dickens's day?

2. In chapter two of Book One, the narrator uses physical description to show the stark contrasts between the dark-eyed, dark-haired Sissy and her fellow student Bitzer whose skin was "unwholesomely deficient in the natural tinge." What does this passage reveal about the narrator's attitude toward Sissy and Bitzer? What does it foreshadow about Bitzer's actions?

3. What is Mr. McChoakumchild's theory of education? What is Dickens's attitude toward this theory? Evaluate the theory in terms of today's students.

4. How do you account for the fact that the facts-only system had different effects on Bitzer, Louisa, Sissy, and young Tom?

5. Why is Sissy omitted from Book Two? Why is Jane included as a character in the novel?

6. How are the children of Coketown treated by adults?

7. How does Dickens depict motherhood in this novel? Why does he depart from the "ideal"?

8. How does Dickens show the process and effects of depersonalization? Were his fears about still further dehumanization by industry warranted? In what ways does society today dehumanize? Are there conditions in this school that dehumanize? What science fiction stories depict the fear of dehumanization? What steps are being taken that extend or soften or halt the dehumanizing aspects

of our world?

9. What does the circus symbolize? Compare the circus people to the Proles in Orwell's *1984*. Can you think of other comparisons in literature, films, and real life?

10. Bitzer reminds Mr. Gradgrind late in the novel that he (Bitzer) was brought up in the catechism that the "whole social system is a question of self-interest." How is that catechism dramatized in the novel? Does that belief prevail today?

WRITING ASSIGNMENTS

During the time needed for reading the novel, I ask students to write briefly at the beginning of class a couple of times a week. Typical assignments: write summary statements for each chapter in the reading assignment; translate into straightforward prose a short passage from the novel; write a personal response to an incident in the novel, such as Sissy's embarrassment at school (students might describe a time when they or a peer experienced humiliation from a teacher or fellow student and draw a conclusion from the incident); write an "insert" for the novel, such as a letter of advice to Rachel and Stephen or to Louisa and James.

In addition to these relatively informal writing assignments, students choose topics from among the following. Several of the discussion questions listed earlier can also be adapted for writing assignments.

1. Two assignments about fathers: a) Write a letter to Thomas Gradgrind telling him how he rates as a father. You might first establish criteria for a good father. b) Was Signor Jupe a "good" or "poor" father? Cite examples and comparisons (with Thomas Gradgrind or other fathers, real or fictional). Can you make use of observations made by other characters in the novel?

2. When Louisa tells her father that she will accept Mr. Bounderby's proposal, she states more than once, "What does it matter?" How does this attitude give her strength? How does it undo her? Interpret her meaning in light of the marriage proposal itself and of the entire novel.

3. Louisa tells her father, "You have been so careful of me that I never had a child's heart." Consider the difference between having a "child's heart" and being "childish." Observe the effects of choking the child's heart in *Hard Times*. Should children behave like adults? Should adults behave like children? How can adults allow the

"child" inside them space to breathe?

4. Archibald MacLeish once wrote, "It is the work of art that creates the human perspective in which information turns to truth." How would Mr. Bounderby respond to this statement? Thomas Gradgrind? Current educators? How do you respond? Find examples that speak to MacLeish's statement.

5. In chapter four of Book Two, the fourth paragraph describes the group as opposed to the individual. A few pages later the narrator comments, "Private feeling must yield to the common cause." Explore this concept, describing times when it is best to "yield to the common cause" and when the individual should prevail.

6. Examine the character of James Harthouse. Why does Dickens include him in his cast of characters? Why doesn't he make him the true hero who rescues the fair maiden? Alternate assignment: write a scene between Louisa and Harthouse that will turn this man with a hollow heart into a genuine hero.

7. In the final chapter Dickens makes quick work of stating that Louisa is destined never to become a loving wife and mother. Why can this never be, according to Dickens? If you were the author, would you have Louisa's life turn out differently? Support Dickens's ending or write a summary of how you would change it.

8. Someone has commented of Dickens's style that he "describes a *smile*, and a *whole man* is recognized by that smile." Explain how Dickens accomplishes such a feat by selecting examples from the novel and showing how details reveal character.

CLASS PROJECTS

In addition to talking and writing about a novel, students enjoy "doing something" with it. The projects described below add a third dimension to the study of Hard Times—and result in some interesting class sessions.

1. Charles Dickens was a journalist and an editor. Divide the class into groups and produce a newspaper with stories, photos, cartoons, ads, lovelorn column, and so on. Use the text of *Hard Times* as your source.

2. Ask each student to develop a set of factual questions, listing the page number for each answer. A student committee then categorizes the questions and arranges them by level of difficulty. These questions become the raw material for a "television" quiz

show. Allow students to work out the format of the show—it'll be more original and entertaining than one you might devise. Videotape the production if possible.

3. Each student makes a chart of the major characters as they appear at the beginning of the novel, arranging them from 1 to 10 on a line labeled "fact" at one end and "fancy" at the other. The student then draws additional lines in a second color to indicate where each character falls on this scale at the end of the novel. Display the charts and develop the following discussion. Which characters moved? Which didn't? Why? Are the characters round or flat, neither, both, or something else? Does it matter?

4. Divide the class into groups. Each group examines the text closely for one of the following items and reports back in a manner that will draw response from the entire class.

    a. Note examples of different "voices" used in this novel. Comment on their function.

    b. Collect and categorize examples of satire and irony (or examples of figures of speech). Are there generalizations to be drawn?

    c. Summarize what each book of the novel is about, commenting on each title. How do the book titles relate to the novel's title? Select several chapter titles to comment on. Finally, make a general observation about Dicken's use of titles.

    d. List names and nicknames of characters and comment on how these names reflect personality. Do they have other functions?

    e. Note descriptions of settings in the country and in the city as well as those on the city's edge What observations can you make?

    f. List all the social criticisms your group can find. Categorize them as part of your presentation.

    g. List literary and historical allusions. Do they burden or enrich the novel?

5. Divide the class into several panels, each of which organizes a discussion or "Meeting of the Minds" program on a topic suggested by the novel. The names below are merely illustrative; many others will serve, including local names. Each character role must be maintained throughout the panel discussion, and each participant submits a biographical sketch to the moderators in advance. For example, the topic *labor unions,* with appearances by Clarence

Darrow, John D. Rockefeller, John L. Lewis, Andrew Carnegie, Walter Reuther, (Slackbridge, Stephen Blackpool, Josiah Bounderby, James Harthouse); or *schools* with Thomas Jefferson, John Dewey, Cotton Mather, Jerome Brunner, John Holt, Horace Mann, Booker T. Washington, members of the local school board (Mr. McChoakumchild, Mr. Bounderby, Mr. Sleary, Rachel). Other topics for which you can provide names from a variety of historical periods and from the novel include women's roles, child rights, environment and industry, social classes, censorship in the schools.

SMALL GROUP OR INDIVIDUAL PROJECTS

The projects outlined below allow you to experiment with a range of formats. Some are risky for a class assignment but ideal for a given individual. All in all, they encourage students to have good times with *Hard Times*.

1. Select scenes for dramatization, oral reading, or mime. You might choose a scene and do a modern counterpart of it or do both the "then" and the "now."
2. Interview people of different ages concerning their experiences with and attitudes toward education (and/or work and leisure). Publish your findings in a pamphlet or present them in a wall chart.
3. Draw or write caricatures of people selected from representative groups in society today--national, state, local, or school. Assign Dickensian names to your characters.
4. Read about the life of Charles Dickens. Present your findings in one of the following ways. a) Deliver a lecture that describes factors in Dickens's life that may have influenced particular ideas, attitudes, characters, and scenes in *Hard Times*. b) Imagine that you are Charles Dickens. Describe in a Dickensian fashion an event of your youth that had lasting impact on your life.
5. Read Studs Terkel's *Hard Times*. How have Dickens and Terkel made the same title relate in different and similar ways to their writings? Consider the major difference between the two works: one is fiction, the other is nonfiction.
6. Read one or more other novels depicting the inequity of treatment of social classes (for example, S. E. Hinton's *The Outsiders*, George Orwell's *1984* or *Animal Farm*, Aldous Huxley's *Brave New World*, Upton Sinclair's *The Jungle*). Prepare an oral report or an essay in

which you make comparisons and draw conclusions.

7. Find examples of poems and/or song lyrics that have de-humanization as their subject. Prepare copies for the class. I lead a discussion of this material, emphasizing similarities and differences between the poems and *Hard Times*.

8. Investigate the art, music, literature, fashion, sports, or architecture of Dickens's time. In what ways do these reflect the times? Do they reinforce what Dickens was commenting on?

9. Recent studies reveal interesting insights in how people are named and how their names affect them. Some change their names. Some women choose to retain their maiden names when they marry. Some investigators argue that names can predict success or failure as well as the type of personality one becomes. Research this topic. Combine what you learn with personal observations and with the way Dickens uses names. Report your most interesting findings to the class. If you like, conduct your own study, using class members as subjects.

Beverly Haley, The Language Works, Fort Morgan, Colorado

Teaching the Epistolary Novel Form

FANNY BURNEY'S *EVELINA*

For several years I have taught Charles Dickens's *Great Expectations* to eighth graders and ninth graders. The formats I use vary, depending on the time allowed and the level of teaching. Yet, after participating in a Louisiana Endowment for the Humanities Summer Institute for Teachers in the summer of 1993 in a course called "The Development of the

English Novel: A (Re)Discovery of Women's Writing," I discovered a woman writer of the eighteenth century whose novel could be taught using the same format that I use to teach Dickens's.

Fanny Burney's *Evelina* is an exceptional book, not only for teaching the epistolary novel form, but also for teaching etiquette, teenage relationships, the "rites of passage" theme, and London society in the eighteenth century.

My students do some journal writing prior to the reading. Topics like the ones below are enjoyable to write about and help the students to identify later with the protagonist's struggles.

Journal Writing Topics

1. Tell about a time when you tried to impress a boy (if you are a girl) or a girl (if you are a boy) in order to either get him or her to notice you or to not look foolish in front of him or her. What happened?

2. Tell about a time when you committed a major social blunder, whether it be at the mall, a dance, at school, on a date, at someone's house, or anywhere. What happened? How did you feel?

3. Tell about a time when you were discovered in public by someone you were trying to impress and you were with a group of people (or even one person) you would rather die than be seen with.

4. Describe the one adult figure you can confide in. What makes this person easy to talk to? Why do you tell this person your deepest fears, dreams, etc.?

5. Were you ever taken advantage of because you were female? young? inexperienced in a particular situation? Describe that situation.

6. What are some lines you use to get a boy or girl to notice you or to go out with you? What works? What doesn't work? Why not?

After discussing these topics in class, I then introduce the students to Fanny Burney and her novel. I explain to the students that most women of the eighteenth century could only write in the epistolary format. Then I give them a little background on attitudes of women writers during that period.

I next hand each student an envelope (in smaller classes students may get two or three envelopes) that has the date of a letter written on it. Inside the envelope is a letter torn from the book *Evelina* and a half sheet of paper with these instructions:

1. Read the letter.
2. On the half sheet of paper (using front and back), write a summary of the letter by briefly telling about the author, audience, plot, characters, and setting. Include any reactions you may have to the contents of the letter.

I give the students a week to complete this assignment at home. During that week, we do small-group research in class on various aspects of London society mentioned in the novel (Drury Lane, St. James Park, Kensington Gardens, balls, theaters, opera, etc.), on the dress and social customs of the eighteenth century, on the music and dance of the period, and on life as a woman writer at the time. Students make visual aids to display in the classroom and report their group findings to the entire class on Friday. Videos of London can also be obtained from the local library. This week of research helps the students to identify further with what they are reading.

The second week the students read and discuss their summaries in class, and we hold discussions on the epistolary form; characterization; themes such as the "rites of passage," social blunders, and initiation into the adult world; London social life; plot; and any other topics that arise. Of course, activities such as character webs, letters written by the students to the characters, character "trees" to show the relationships among the characters, and other writing exercises can be incorporated into this week's discussions.

Next I divide the students into small groups and have them discuss key ideas from the novel. The small groups then discuss their findings with the entire class.

I find this method successful, especially with slower readers and junior high students, because it exposes them to literature they may not otherwise read and it allows us to cover a long and perhaps difficult novel in a short period. (For example, I may teach *Great Expectations* in the same format by dividing the book as Dickens wrote it, giving each student three consecutive chapters such that each third chapter ends in a "cliffhanger." The students love seeing the book being torn apart. We study Dickens's writing methods and put the book back together again at the end of this study.)

This unit may also be used to introduce other epistolary novels such as *Pamela* or *The Color Purple*, or to illustrate how history is preserved in people's letters. You might even have the students begin keeping a letter-style journal for a month or so and then combine those letters that were "written" to friends, parents, or other relatives into the student's own "novella."

At the end of our *Evelina* unit, the students enjoy a word puzzle as a review. They also enjoy participating in a "British Tea," for which the students bring refreshments such as scones, shortbread, jam, tea, etc. We have quite a class party.

Mary F. Sianjina, Lee Junior High School, Monroe, Louisiana

WINNING WITH WUTHERING HEIGHTS

If you're looking for a few new angles on teaching an old classic, here are some intriguing ideas for class discussion and writing.

1. Show your students the classic 1939 Samuel Goldwyn film starring Laurence Olivier, Merle Oberon, and David Niven. It's very helpful in getting students to see the events, setting, and characters. The movie only dramatizes half the novel, providing a perfect opportunity for prediction and speculation. Ask students if they think the second half of the novel could be filmed effectively, and why or why not. If the second half were to be filmed, what incidents and dialogues might be highlighted? You might also ask students to consider who would be cast in a modern film version of the novel.

2. After students watch the 1939 film, ask them to consider and write on the following questions:

    Should this movie be colorized?
    What would be added or taken away?
    Compare Laurence Olivier and Merle Oberon to your expectations of how they should have looked.

How does the music used in the film affect your viewing of it? Is the music effective?

What was left out of the movie version of the novel that you think should have been filmed? For each scene that you think should have been included in the film, discuss several different ways in which the scene might have been filmed. (Consider lighting, camera angles, director's instructions to the cast, and so on.)

In what ways does the movie change the death scene of Catherine? Was the movie's ending effective? Why or why not? Was it too sentimental? Why or why not?

3. If you are able to find other versions of *Wuthering Heights*, you can show students how various other artists responded to the major themes and characters of Brontë's novel. Some of the more interesting possibilities for comparison and contrast are Randolph Carter's 1933 play version of the novel, available from Baker's Plays in Boston (100 Chauncy Street, Boston, MA 02111); the 1971 British movie version, starring Timothy Dalton as Heathcliff; Kate Bush's song "Wuthering Heights," available on Pat Benatar's *Crimes of Passion* album; and Sylvia Plath's poem "Wuthering Heights," included in her book *Crossing the Water* (Harper and Row, 1980).

4. You might also ask students to read and compare the contemporary reviews of *Wuthering Heights* with later and modern reviews and criticism of the novel. Two possible sources are Thomas C. Moser's *Wuthering Heights: Text, Sources, Criticism* (Harcourt, Brace and World, 1962) and the Norton Critical Edition of the novel, edited by William M. Sale, Jr. (Second Edition, W. W. Norton, 1972).

Gary Kerley, Brenau Academy, Gainesville, Georgia

ALLUSIONS IN THE MAYOR OF CASTERBRIDGE

W hen first preparing to teach Thomas Hardy's *The Mayor of Casterbridge,* I was struck by its wealth of allusions and disheartened to realize that all but the most obvious would be missed by twelfth graders. In teaching any literature written before 1975, we encounter references which high school students, raised on *Batman* and *Peanuts,* simply don't get. Dictionaries help, but they seldom encourage the student to dig beyond a surface interpretation. This assignment challenges students not only to use the reference section, but to read closely and to analyze the resultant information on at least two levels. Most important of all, the students learn *how* allusions work within texts; this understanding enriches their future reading.

The Mayor of Casterbridge provides an excellent opportunity to show students the many ways in which allusions may inform and enrich a text. During our study of the novel I define the term and point out that Hardy's readers shared a common body of information, including history, ancient myth and legend, Shakespeare, and the Bible. As part of our preparation, I read them the story of King Saul in I Samuel and we draw the obvious parallels to Michael Henchard's fall. I then point out the allusion to Saul in chapter 26 and the choir's discussion of David in chapter 33. The class begins to see that allusion can be more than literary metaphor or simile, that a knowledge of the stories that Hardy refers to almost casually can add depth and resonance to the entire novel. (This is not a religion lesson; present it as literature, legend, or history. It works on all levels.)

I assign one allusion (or one pair of allusions) from the handout (see page 119) to each student. Even after eliminating the least resonant and interesting, there are plenty to go around. The wide variety allows me to match the difficulty of the allusion with the ability of the student, a real benefit in heterogeneous classes.

The assignment is divided into three distinct parts, each requiring a different skill. Part I, which must be documented, is to identify the allusion and to explain briefly but clearly exactly what it refers to. For example, "I, Cain, go alone" alludes to Cain's banishment after he killed his brother Abel. A summary of the Genesis story, including a hint of motivation and characterization, would complete Part I. This is probably the only time all year that I allow students to write plot summary, but an accurate paraphrase of a complex story can be a challenge. The library staff loves the challenge; they do prove their often ignored boast that they can find literally anything. If forewarned, they will virtually eliminate the wail, "I've looked everywhere; it can't be found." Students discover and use references they never knew existed, including Bible concordances and dictionaries of literary characters. Sharing sources and leads is encouraged. One class period in the library and a quick review of the *MLA Handbook* should complete this section.

Part II is the heart of the assignment. Students explain how the allusion works: what exactly is being compared to what. For example, they see that Henchard is like Cain because he is an outcast from his home and family. His jealousy and impetuousness have led him into a crime others consider unforgivable. A close reading of several pages before and after the allusion are essential here. More literal-minded students may require coaching. Just explaining what they have found to a friend can provide a breakthrough. Most experience an exhilarating moment of discovery. Once they have identified and understood the allusion, Hardy's point is made.

Part III is the least scholarly but often the most creative part of the paper. Students relate the allusion to the novel as a whole, considering how it illuminates character, provides an ironic contrast, or reinforces a theme. To do this, they must have a good grasp of both the novel and the allusion and be able to analyze possible connections between the two. In the above example, a student may notice the ironic twist Hardy gives to the biblical story: Cain may have denied he was his brother's keeper, but "Abel" Whittle keeps his brother faithfully. Some have compared Henchard's crime to Cain's, concluding that Hardy was more harsh than God himself. Part III may produce anything from scholarly insight to delightful flights of fancy to drivel. But every student goes beyond the analysis found in *Cliffs Notes* and learns to rely a little more on his or her ability to read closely and interpret what is being read.

This assignment requires considerable teacher preparation. (Don't march the class to the library until you have some idea of where you can find each allusion; the most knowledgeable and obliging librarians would rebel.) But the results are worth the effort. Every paper is different. They are short and specific and therefore quick to grade, but they are imaginative and creative too. And, since allusions are everywhere, we begin to keep a constantly changing display of cartoons, ads, and newspaper headlines. Hagar the Horrible comments on *Beowulf,* Allied Van Lines quotes Keats, *The Post* steals from Oscar Wilde. Students love it when they suddenly "get" a Far Side cartoon on *Hamlet.* It's one of the joys of being literate.

After completing the assignment, I ask students to try an allusion or two in their journals. I've been unjustly but creatively compared to both Mr. Gradgrind and Lady Macbeth. One girl revealed that homework was her albatross, and several have found their own Tintern Abbeys while walking on the beach. Like metaphors or periodic sentences, allusions are a tool young writers can learn to appreciate in the works of others and can use to enrich their own prose. And through their work with allusions, students discover their ability to research, analyze, and interpret literature.

Andrea E. McNally, Cardinal Newman High School, West Palm Beach, Florida

ALLUSIONS IN *THE MAYOR OF CASTERBRIDGE*

Thomas Hardy expected his readers to be familiar with history, Shakespeare, ancient myths and legends, and, most important, the Bible. He used carefully chosen allusions to all of these to create mood, illuminate character, and point out ironies in situations.

You will be assigned one allusion from the list below. You must do three specific things with this allusion:

I.   Research: Answer the questions "Who?" "What?" and "When?" Summarize in a paragraph or two the complete factual background of the allusion. To what *exactly* is Hardy referring? Part I must be documented according to MLA standards.

II.   Answer the question "Why?" In a paragraph or two, relate this specific allusion to the scene or situation in which it is used. Be sure to read carefully the entire section in which the allusion appears so that you get the whole picture.

III.   Speculate on the wider implications of the allusion. How might it relate to the novel as a whole? Does an understanding of this allusion contribute to an understanding of the theme of the novel? Does it influence the mood? Does it help to reveal character? Feel free to be creative. And, if your allusion has two parts, be sure to comment on the connection or similarities between the two.

(Page numbers refer to the Signet Classic paperback edition, 1980, New York: The New American Library.)

The Allusions

1.   "Ye may as well look for manna-food" (p. 37)
2.   as from the unseen hands of Cranstoun's Goblin Page (p. 67)
3.   like the quicker cripple at Bethesda (p. 72)
4a. a gazing legion of Hadrian's soldiery (p. 77)
 b. coins of Hadrian, Posthumus, and the Constantines (p. 135)
5.   the education of Achilles (p. 81)
6.   like leafy Laocoöns (p. 82)
7a. "like Job, I could curse the day that gave me birth" (p. 83)
 b. like a less scrupulous Job (p. 281)
8.   as high as the gates of Solomon's Temple (p. 96)
9.   the prophet Baruch's sly definition: . . . (p. 99)
10. as if Nature had been advised by Correggio in their creation (p. 109)
11. Like Jacob in Padan-Aram (p. 117)
12. as Faust has been described (p. 117)
13a. Romeo part (p. 117)
 b. some much-courted Adonis (p. 221)
14. like Bellerophon (p. 118)
15. like the brethren at the avowal of Joseph (p. 125)
16. Like Prester John's, his table has been spread, and infernal harpies had snatched up the food (p. 128)
17a. as Minerva's own (p. 132)
 b. the serene Minerva-eyes (p. 323)
18. Like the Princess Ida (p. 132)
19a. as the avenues of Karnac (p. 135)
 b. as Pharaoh's chariots (p. 262)
20. Austerlitz (p. 136)
21. a well-known conception of Titian's (p. 151)
22. the weak Apostle at the accusation, "Thy speech bewrayeth thee!" (p. 152)
23a. Dan Cupid's magnet (p. 160)
 b. Aphrodite ever spoke thus (p. 242)
24. "so that some falls by the wayside and some among thorns" (p. 168)
25. "'He that observeth the wind shall not sow,' so the Preacher said" (p. 168)
26. the two disciples supping at Emmaus . . . like the evangelist who had to write it down (P. 179-80)
27. as the Alastor of those households whose crime it was to be poor (p. 182)
28. like Saul at his reception by Samuel (p. 184)
29. "like living in Revelations" (p. 185)
30a. to follow the triumphal chariot of this man to the Capitol (p. 189)
 b. his Calpurnia (p. 262)
31. Shallow and Silence themselves (p. 197)
32. with Abrahamic success (p. 203)
33. Yahoo antics and gestures (p. 203)
34. like John Gilpin (p. 210)
35. like the poet Ovid (note: see if you can get the Latin quote translated) (p. 212)
36. in Nathan tones (p. 213)
37. "Yes; she was wise, she was wise in her generation!" (p. 226)
38. "Psalm the Hundred-and-Ninth" . . . "Servant David" (p. 230)
39. Rosalind's exclamation: "Mistress, know yourself; . . . a good man's love" (p. 232)
40. as Tamerlane's trumpet (p. 241)
41. the Adullam of all the surrounding villages (p. 251)
42. like Ashton at the disappearance of Ravenswood (p. 253)
43. like the crew of *Comus* (p.277)
44. plumes, like those of Juno's bird, and set with Argus eyes (p. 297)
45. "I—Cain—go alone as I deserve" (p. 307)
46. as a Samson shorn (p. 316)
47. the returned Crusoe (p. 321)
48. the Capharaum (p. 326)

A PREREADING EXERCISE FOR *LORD OF THE FLIES*

Williiam Golding's popular novel *Lord of the Flies* is taught today in many high schools, according to the Center for the Learning and Teaching of Literature. I teach the novel to eleventh graders of average ability. Before we begin reading, students participate in a prereading activity that focuses on a "what-if" situation taken from the novel's plot.

I begin the activity by asking the entire class to form one large circle. I remain outside the circle and, after giving directions, do not enter into the conversation at all.

I tell students that they are going to read a novel about a group of boys stranded on an island. I mention that I would first like to see how my students would handle things and then later we can compare their ideas with the ideas of the boys in the novel.

The scenario and directions are simple:

1. You are on a desert island. The island has a mountainous area, a forest, a sandy beach, and a lagoon.
2. There are no adults left in your group. The pilot, co-pilot, navigator, and attendants have all perished in the crash. No one in the circle, however, is seriously injured.
3. The plane has drifted out to sea.
4. You have only the items on your person and the clothes on your back, nothing else.
5. Your job is to organize to survive.

Helping students set up in a circle and giving directions takes about five minutes. I tell students they have twenty to twenty-five minutes to organize.

Then I don't speak to students again until I call "time."

At first, students usually just sit in place and smile at one another waiting for someone to take charge and tell them what to do. The class leader then starts organizing and most students then begin to participate. Just as in the class setting, the more reticent students do not speak.

My job is to sit on the outside of the circle and take notes on everything that is said in the allotted time. When time is up, I read the transcript of group conversation back to the students, often amidst much laughter, and ask them to reflect on what just happened. I ask pointed questions: Who was the leader? How was he or she selected? Were you happy with this person as leader? Is this person also the class leader? What did you decide to do first? How were the chores divided? What did you forget to accomplish? What would you add or change? What other roles did people play? Would you have survived?

Some results are startling. In one class the women's movement was set back 500 years. The boys made all the decisions and took upon themselves the tasks of hunting, fishing, and protecting, whereas the girls were ordered to clean and cook the food and clean up the campsite. Remarkably, the girls agreed!

Some groups became militaristic and created a complex system of rules and punishments. In one class, students adopted a rule requiring three days of ostracism for stealing food or personal belongings.

Another group became fervent followers of Darwin and kept reiterating the idea of "survival of the fittest." I played the devil's advocate during the discussion and asked, "What about helping each other to gather food or taking care of each other during illnesses?" However, I couldn't soften students' theories. A few boys told me that in order to survive one had to be tough and cold-hearted. (I assured them I would use this philosophy when it came time to grade essay tests!)

Yet another class turned out to be the most organized and democratic. A girl and boy were voted co-leaders. They then proceeded to list chores—scout the island, pick berries, make shelters, create weapons, find water—and asked for volunteers for each of those activities. The group cooperated well and systematically went about colonizing their island. They even set time aside for sunbathing. When I asked them if they thought they could survive a real experience similar to this, their emphatic answer was *yes.* I believed them.

With the remaining time, I asked students to critique the exercise. Most classes said they enjoyed the opportunity to work without being directed by the teacher. Most students found the activity to be fun and informative and agreed that it should be done again with other classes. Most were anxious to see what the boys in Golding's novel would do. Students' comments provided a natural segue into their first assignment: to read the first chapter of *Lord of the Flies,* make a list of what the boys in the novel do, and compare and contrast the novel's characters' behaviors to those of the class members.

This exercise allows students to make rational decisions and value judgments, to think critically and creatively, and to reflect on ways in which, as human beings, they are both independent and dependent. Of course, it's ultimately an exercise in make-believe—as one student pointed out, "We're not on a desert island. We're in Room 205"—but it's an exercise that makes Golding's novel and characters real to students, and at the same time brings students to interesting realizations about themselves.

Regina Rudolph, Hightstown High School, Hightstown, New Jersey

ANIMAL FARM: DIRECTIONS FOR DISCUSSION

Of all the novels taught in junior high and high school, George Orwell's *Animal Farm* is one of the least likely to suffer "the silent treatment" at students' hands. Students generally have heated responses to the events of the story; they can find a lot to say even before they fully understand the novel's symbolism and deeper levels of meaning.

One way to proceed after students have read *Animal Farm* is to lead a general class discussion of the novel's allegorical meaning and then to let small groups meet to discuss more specific questions. After several days of group discussion (and further reading or research, if necessary), a chairperson or recorder presents the group's responses to the rest of the class. This approach encourages participation, requires that students delve a little deeper into the novel, and gives everyone the benefit of each group's thoughts and answers.

Listed below are examples of questions that could be used to direct group discussion. These examples are grouped loosely by the topics of characterization, literary devices and figures of speech, and satire. Other questions might be devised to cover other topics. The number of questions assigned to each group can vary depending on the difficulty of the questions and on how much time students are given to prepare their responses.

Characterization

Which animals seem most like human beings?

Do you know people like Molly? like Boxer? like Benjamin? What are the main traits of these characters?

What is the author's point in having the sheep chant, "Four legs good, two legs bad"?

What are "developing" characters? Who are the developing characters in the novel? What are "static" characters? Who are the static characters in the novel?

Do you think the novel would be as effective if the characters were people instead of animals? Explain why or why not.

Literary Devices and Figures of Speech

What do the sheep stand for?

Why does the author choose sheep to chant the Revolutionists' motto?

Find and explain other examples of symbolism in the novel.

Explain the significance of these names: Snowball, Napoleon, Squealer, Mr. Whymper.

Find examples of similes and metaphors.

Satire

Why were the puppies raised in secret by Napoleon?

How are young people indoctrinated in communist or fascist societies?

Give examples of "brainwashing" from the text. Compare these examples with brainwashing techniques in past and present society.

Compare brainwashing to peer pressure.

Compare the distortion of events with distortion of news by public officials or the press.

What is "rationalization"? What examples of rationalization do you find in the novel? In what way does our society rationalize wrongdoing? How do we rationalize in our everyday conduct?

Rosemary Gelshenen, Norman Thomas High School, New York, New York

6 | EMPHASIS: NINETEENTH-CENTURY AMERICAN NOVELS

CONNECTING TO
THE SCARLET LETTER

Each year at our school the word is passed down to the sophomore class from older students that *The Scarlet Letter* is difficult, boring, and incomprehensible. So when these students begin their junior year, many of their minds are already closed to Nathaniel Hawthorne's classic novel. I approached this unit determined to illuminate the Puritan period for these students by having them relate to the emotions that almost all teenagers have experienced to some degree or another: guilt, loneliness, and alienation.

To help make the connection, I had the students select a novel from the following list of contemporary novels, some more than others ideally suited to young adult readers. Students were asked to keep journals of their reactions to the novel of their choice.

Summer of My German Soldier—Bette Greene
The Water is Wide—Pat Conroy
The Great Santini—Pat Conroy
The Lords of Discipline—Pat Conroy
Slake's Limbo—Felice Holman
Father Figure—Richard Peck
A Day No Pigs Would Die—Richard Peck
Remembering the Good Times—Richard Peck
Ghosts I Have Been—Richard Peck
Close Enough to Touch—Richard Peck
Killing Mr. Griffin—Lois Duncan
I Am the Cheese—Robert Cormier
The Chocolate War—Robert Cormier
Beyond the Chocolate War—Robert Cormier
After the First Death—Robert Cormier
Stotan!—Chris Crutcher
Running Loose—Chris Crutcher
Crazy Horse Electric Game—Chris Crutcher

Notes for Another Life—Sue E. Bridgers
Home Before Dark—Sue E. Bridgers
Taking Terri Mueller—Norma F. Mazer
Night Kites—M.E. Kerr
Little Little—M.E. Kerr
Tiger Eyes—Judy Blume
Cold Sassy Tree—Olive A. Burns
The War Between the Classes—Gloria D. Miklowitz
The Day the Senior Class Got Married—Gloria D. Miklowitz

The students jotted down comments and impressions in their journals as they read each night. Then they went back and reread their comments and looked with a critical eye for examples of guilt, alienation, and loneliness. They searched for how characters illustrated these themes. They thought about which characters they were empathetic towards and why. They commented on what parts of the plot confused or interested them. They looked for what did or didn't develop the way they thought it would, and generally noted anything else they wanted to discuss further. Class discussions were based on their entries. Finally, they wrote an essay analyzing these themes from their novel and shared those at a Reading Round Table.

When we finally began *The Scarlet Letter,* the students felt empowered to read critically this once-dreaded novel. After reading their journals, it was obvious that they had become personally involved with their characters. One student wrote in response to Chapter 13,

> This is great. All this tension is mounting; all the strings are entwined, and the stage is set. Now all that has to be done is the climax. Dimmey is going to spill the beans and I'm going to have a front row seat! Pearl sure is thirsty for recognition in public by Dimmey. Why??

With this kind of personal connection to *The Scarlet Letter,* students found the required essays much easier to write. They drew ideas for a thesis from their journals, and then extracted the necessary support for their papers. Lively group discussions gave the students more "food for thought," and the culminating Reading Round Table was filled with students who

128

really cared about what they wrote. We finished the unit feeling that we had all gained insight into the Puritan period.

Jeannine S. Hirtle, McCullough High School, McCullough, Texas

ENTERING INTO THE SPIRIT OF THE TIMES

The Scarlet Letter may be initially intimidating to students who are unused to Hawthorne's language and unfamiliar with Puritan times. However, first reluctance often gives way to enthusiasm as the mood of the story draws students in. A preliminary assignment such as the following one can help to create a relaxed atmosphere for reading and discussion, while at the same time introducing the Puritan attitudes portrayed in *The Scarlet Letter.*

This prereading assignment is a spontaneous enactment of "Endicott and the Red Cross." Spontaneous, that is, for the students! In advance, I assemble and prepare the props that will transform the class into Puritan members of the Salem community that defied Archbishop Laud and the Royalists in the 1630s–1640s. I find that, after their performance, the class is better able to understand the rigid and righteous mentality that condemned Hester Prynne and shunned her and Pearl. "Endicott" also provides us with the first image of "a young woman, with no mean share of beauty, whose doom it was to wear the letter A on the breast of her gown, in the eyes of the world . . . ."

"Endicott" is a very short story of five paperback pages. (It is included in the back of the Signet Classic edition of *The Scarlet Letter* which many schools use.) Basically, the enactment is my reading of the story with the students responding to the directions of the narrative. (I do the reading so that I can cue students at the appropriate moments.) I begin by telling students that we will spend one class period getting in the mood to read *The Scarlet Letter*. I then describe the various speaking parts, assign students to the parts, and hand out props and lines. Each character's name is printed on a cardboard tag attached to yarn that hangs from the neck. (Paper sheets scotch-taped to the students also work, but the cardboard tags last from year to year and never come off during the enactment.) Essential characters are Endicott, Roger Williams, the Episcopalian, the Royalist, the Female Gossip, the Wanton Gospeller, and the Young Woman with the Scarlet A. The remainder of the class can be designated as militiamen, "stately Indians," and villagers. For a feeling of total class involvement, it is important for every student to wear a designation.

Props can vary according to what is on hand. I have access to the school play closet, so on my list are the following: a frame booth that functions as the pillory and stocks, a feathered Cavalier hat for the Royalist, feathers for the Indians, swords for Endicott and the militia, gray hard hats that make wonderful soldiers' helmets for the militia, a high-crowned Puritan hat and black cape for Roger Williams, a scarf for the flag, cotton swabs or a carrot to stick in the mouth of the Wanton Gospeller, and a large red construction-paper "A."

After name tags and props have been distributed, I distribute lines to the five characters who have something to say in the story. Each student's list of spoken parts is typed and backed with stiff construction paper. Endicott speaks eight times, and I designate each as Speech 1, Speech 2, and so on. Roger Williams speaks three times, the others only once. For example, on the Royalist's sheet are his only words: *"Treason!! Treason!! He Hath Defaced The King's Banner!!!"* The Wanton Gospeller says, *"Call You This Liberty of Conscience?"* When the time comes for the characters to speak, I prompt, "Endicott, Speech 3," or "Episcopalian, speak your words now fervently!"

The enactment is accomplished in one class hour, the kids love it, and ad-libbing ensues; the mood is set for our foray into Puritan times. I appreciate how preferable a dramatic, student-involving introduction is to a soporific reading of "The Custom House." As a matter of fact, I save that until *after* we have finished the novel!

Rosemary Laughlin, University High School, Urbana, Illinois

PEARL'S CUSTODY HEARING

A stimulating and thought-provoking activity to enrich Hawthorne's *The Scarlet Letter* is a custody hearing over Pearl.

This activity works best after chapter six, when Hester goes to the governor's mansion to plead to keep Pearl. The length of the activity can vary depending on how many witnesses are called to testify. In my class, the custody hearing was held over five class periods of forty-two minutes each. The prosecution and defense both had two days to present their cases. The last day was set aside for the judge's decision, a vote by the entire class to see how a jury might have voted, and a discussion and evaluation of the entire activity.

My classes were small—fifteen students—so everyone had a role. Basically, the cast of characters includes: a judge, who makes the final ruling; a prosecutor, who is working for the church and who wants custody of Pearl; a defense attorney, who is hired by Hester; various witnesses such as Hester, Rev. Dimmesdale, Pearl, Chillingworth, Gov. Bellingham; a social worker, whose job it is to give the most objective testimony; various and sundry people of the town, such as the church deacon, the older vicious women of the town, the younger sympathetic women, and the town jailer.

The two most demanding roles are those of the prosecutor and the defense attorney. They have to organize and prep their witnesses, prepare and deliver opening and closing statements, and be perceptive enough to take notes during each other's direct questioning, and then turn around the witness's testimony during cross-examination. If there are enough students, the teacher may want to have assistant prosecutors and defense attorneys to assist in the note-taking and strategy planning.

These should stay in character as much as possible and answer as a seventeenth-century Puritan would. For this purpose students should review the text of *The Scarlet Letter* in order to answer any questions. One amusing witness proved to be Pearl, who answered in a childlike voice, dressed in a

Puritan-style cap. Hester also caused a sensation when she appeared in a black dress with a construction-paper "A" on her chest. The judge also appeared in costume, wearing a borrowed chorus robe.

I set up the classroom to resemble a courtroom as much as possible by having the defense on one side, the prosecution on the other, the judge up front at the teacher's desk, and a court bailiff who swore in each witness. The judge entered and left the room as he would have in a real court hearing, and the entire court stood as he came and went. If it's possible, prior to the classroom hearing, the students may want to watch a TV court drama—*L. A. Law* or *Matlock*, for example—just to view courtroom protocol and the sequence of events.

The results of class cases can be very different. In one class the students voted to give custody of Pearl to Hester; in the other class they voted to give the church custody of Pearl. The judge in both classes, however, gave custody of Pearl to Hester. One judge even added various stipulations: Hester must bring Pearl to church every Sunday, and Pearl must be tested in her knowledge of the catechism in three months.

Here are some guidelines to make this activity successful:

1. Students need to be capable of investing thought and time in role playing. Previous experience with role playing is helpful.

2. Classroom discussion early on will help to clarify each student's role. Let students brainstorm what they know about courtroom procedure and the responsibilities of each participant; supplement this with information from other sources (for example, the encyclopedia entry on "Legal Procedure"). As the various tasks and roles take shape, they can be listed on the chalkboard. A partial list might look something like this:

   Judge: listens to evidence, sustains or overrules attorney's, sometimes calls the attorneys into chambers to question or reprimand, decides case

   Prosecuting Attorney/Defense Attorney: prepares witnesses, examines and cross-examines witnesses, presents opening and closing statements

3. Review courtroom protocol ahead of time so that everyone knows what to expect and can help contribute to a realistic courtroom scene.

   Students will probably want to include such details as they

remember from courtroom dramas they have read and watched on television: the bailiff's calling "All rise" when the judge enters; the bailiff's call to order ("This court will now come to order" or "This court is now in session"); the judge's use of the gavel to quiet the courtroom; the proper responses of the various parties during the calling and swearing in of witnesses; the judge's stating, "The witness may now step down," at the appropriate time; and so on.

4. Worksheets can help students to organize information in preparation for the trial. The students in the roles of prosecuting attorney and defense attorney will find worksheets especially useful. A worksheet for the prosecuting attorney, for example, might list a general description of necessary tasks, a checklist of tasks completed, and provide space for writing witnesses' names, questions to ask the witnesses, notes on the evidence witnesses are expected to give, main points of opening and closing statements, etc.

Worksheets may be made up ahead of time or drafted by the class during discussion and brainstorming.

All in all, this was an exciting, stimulating activity which my students highly recommended for future classes. This activity brought *The Scarlet Letter* to life and made Hawthorne relevant to the twentieth century.

Regina Rudolph, Hightstown High School, Hightstown, New Jersey

Confronting Controversy in the Classroom

HUCKLEBERRY FINN

Last year, in the midst of teaching *The Adventures of Huckleberry Finn* to my eleventh graders, the controversy over whether or not *Huckleberry Finn* should be banned from the classroom made news in our state.[1]

An editorial in the local newspaper summed up the frequency of this debate when it began, "Here we go again . . . ."[2] This time it seemed that Mr. John Wallace, an administrative aide at, ironically, Mark Twain Intermediate School in Fairfax County, Virginia, objected to the book saying that "It's damaging to black students, and that's been proven beyond a shadow of a doubt."[3] Mr. Wallace, who is himself black, went on to say, "Anybody who teaches this book is a racist."[4]

I, however, disagreed with Mr. Wallace's assertion. Aside from the entertainment and stylistic values of the book, I wanted my students to realize that *The Adventures of Huckleberry Finn* addresses many of the same social issues that we face today. Violence, racism, and hypocrisy are far from extinct in the modern world, and while the students recognized the superiority of the character of Jim, as well as many other ironies in the novel, they failed to give any more than cursory notice to the novel's relevance to their own lives. Furthermore, they were quick to discard Mr. Wallace's complaints as "ridiculous," feeling confident that I would agree. Although I did agree with much of what the students said, I could not help but notice how totally unconcerned they were with a view other than their own. As far as they were concerned, Mark Twain was not a racist and their teacher obviously agreed with them, or she would not have assigned the book as required reading. No further discussion was needed!

I told the class that the next day they would informally debate someone who did not agree with them, someone who believed *Huckleberry Finn* should definitely be banned from any required reading list, and that they should be prepared to defend their position by (1) discussing the issue with their parents, other adults, and their peers and (2) reading and taking notes from at least one newspaper or magazine article related to the issue of censorship in the public schools. Because they were in unanimous agreement, the debate would involve all of them against a lone opponent.

The following day I walked into class introducing myself as Mr. John Wallace. Since I had saved several articles regarding the controversy and since I had seen Mr. Wallace interviewed on television, I felt that I could, indeed, do his side justice. I gave a brief statement of my position and invited a student to do the same for his position. I then requested questions from the class. It didn't take long for me to fall into the role I was playing, nor did it take long for the students to respond to me as John Wallace. The initially rather condescending tone of the class made it evident that they intended to make "short work" of Mr. John Wallace by patiently showing him the "obvious" errors in his thinking.

"Mr. Wallace, don't you think that you're being somewhat overly sensitive to the language used in *Huckleberry Finn?* After all, Mark Twain is only showing us his view of reality," deigned one student. When I cited the number of times Mark Twain used the work "nigger" (189)[5] in the novel, other students were quick to come back with statements concerning "authenticity" and "the vernacular of the day," all very legitimate responses.

The quick tempo of the class abruptly ceased, however, when I asked if it was morally right to include literature in the school curriculum which crushed the spirit of the students that it was supposed to enrich. The unity of opinion suddenly disintegrated amidst a collage of enigmatic faces, each beginning to look within himself for the first time since the discussion had begun. Like kernels of popcorn on a hot stove, ideas started to flower and hands popped up, slowly at first and then quickly one after another.

"If you ask me, anyone who can't see that Mark Twain meant to show that slavery was a terrible institution just doesn't *want* to see it. After all, the really bad characters are all white—Pap, the slave traders, and even the Duke and King," said a girl in the front row.

"Then why does he make Jim an illiterate fool?" asked a boy in the back.

"He isn't a fool," replied the girl. "Anything foolish he did was because of circumstances he couldn't control. Jim knew that Tom's elaborate plan to escape from the Phelps' plantation was ridiculous since all Jim had to do was walk out the door, but because Tom was white, Jim had to go along with his plan. Tom was the fool, not Jim."

The only black male student in the class then entered the conversation. "If Mark Twain was a racist, he never would have had Jim save Tom's life at the end of the book. Jim didn't know that he had been freed in Miss Watson's will. As far as he knew, he was giving up his freedom to save Tom Sawyer's life, not because Tom was white nor because he was even particularly close to Tom, but because Tom was a human being. Isn't that the message of the book: that we all share a common bond of humanity regardless of color. The book doesn't crush my spirit; in fact, Jim makes me feel really good about being black."

Still in the guise of John Wallace, I told the class how I had felt, the only black child in my English class, when the teacher read aloud, the word 'nigger' cutting deeper and deeper into my self-esteem each time It was read. And when my classmates laughed at Jim's slave dialect, I knew they were also laughing at me.

A black girl quickly joined in telling the class about the confusion she felt when, as a kindergarten student, a playmate called her a "nigger." She went on to say that when she first heard the word read aloud in class from the novel, it made her uncomfortable, but she realized that it was just a word, a word that would have been accepted in Huck's time and place. "That doesn't make it a good word," she said, "but pretending it wasn't used would be a lie."

The discussion continued with still another student pointing out that racist remarks are with us today just as they were in Mark Twain's day. "Other authors have used derogatory language to get their points across. Richard Wright and William Faulkner both used the word 'nigger' in their stories, but not to show that blacks were inferior to whites. They wanted us to see the limitations that society has put on black people so that we would do something about it. Maybe Mark Twain was trying to do the same thing."

Then the quietest girl in class raised her hand to ask, "Mr. Wallace, you object to the racist language in *Huckleberry Finn*, but how can you change something that's wrong with society unless people realize that it's wrong?" She explained that in her sociology class she had learned that before positive change can occur, people have to recognize the wrongs in society and confront them.

The really important thing that was happening, however, was not exactly what the students were saying, but rather that each of the forty-five students in that classroom was thinking, not merely recording and reciting. My students were truly involved in an active exchange of thoughtful, perceptive, and original ideas. They no longer dismissed Mr. Wallace's arguments as inconsequential; they listened and responded with sensitivity.

I cannot say that the opinions of the students were greatly altered by this debate. Most stood firm in their belief that *Huckleberry Finn* was an indictment of racism, rather that a racist novel; a few were not quite as sure as they had been before the debate, and no one could unequivocally accept the notion that Mark Twain was a racist. What did change, however, were the attitudes of my students. They had defended their position against someone who had sincerely and intelligently disagreed with them, and in doing so they were "forced" to listen to, not merely hear, what "Mr. Wallace" had said. They also had to carefully select and organize their own ideas and then verbalize them. As a result of this process, their initial self-righteous myopia was transformed into a greater understanding of their own ideas and a respect for those of other people.

Another change which occurred as a result of the debate was that of increased motivation. One boy who admitted that he had never read a book in its entirety finished and even participated in several follow-up activities. Both teacher and student-initiated projects resulted from this discussion.

Not all students participated in each of the activities, but everyone was required to complete at least one of them. Although students should be given specific instructions and requirements for each project, these details will vary according to the available resources, and they should, therefore, be determined by individual teachers. The following is a list of activities which I found most successful:

1. One student group made a video tape of their version of "Meet the Press" with students assuming the roles of moderator, panel members, and guest, Mark Twain. The panel queried Mr. Twain on his views concerning the controversy surrounding his book.

2. Students selected a scene from the novel and put it in script form. They then wrote an original script set in modern times which paralleled the events from the first scene and which illustrated the similarities between the social concerns of Mark Twain's time and those of today's society.

3. Students wrote letters to the editors of school, local, and out-of-town newspapers concerning censorship in public schools.

4. Students wrote letters expressing their ideas on censorship to members of school boards in areas where *Huckleberry Finn* had come under attack (Fairfax County, Va.; Waukegan, Ill.; Chicago, Ill.).

5. A member of the community spoke to the class about her experience in the civil rights marches of the 1960s. A student taped her speech and started an oral library for the class. At the end of the year, he left his library of tapes with me, and my students this year have continued to add to it.

6. Students compiled scrapbooks of newspaper and magazine articles related to the issue of censorship.

7. Students kept two-week journals in which they wrote from the point of view of a modern Huck Finn traveling across the country. The journal included local color describing the people, the areas, and the events with which the narrator came in contact.

My students were not the only ones to learn from this confrontation with controversy. While I pretended to be John Wallace, passionately explaining how it felt to be the lone black student forced to listen to white teachers, to read "white textbooks," and silently to accept white society, I was transported to a time when I was fifteen sitting in class next to Mary, the only black student in a very alien environment. I sat beside Mary for an entire school year never understanding why my attempts at "kindness" were rebuffed, never seeing beyond the stoic, cold stare of her black eyes. Now, after twenty years, I could finally understand. It was not until I sought to expand the peripheral vision of my own students, not until I consciously sought to "walk in the shoes" of John Wallace, that I could begin to discern the enigma of Mary's "indifference." She was an outsider; I was an insider. Mary recognized my "beneficence" for what it was, the patronizing prattle of someone unable to see beyond her own narrow world.

Indeed, Mary was right; I was much too content in my own world to want to venture beyond it, and I certainly was never challenged to do so in school. Quite the contrary. It was far safer to discuss the importance of daily life in "Our Town" or to scrutinize the beauty of a Grecian urn than it was to come face to face with an issue that confronted all of us every day, especially if that issue made us uncomfortable. Perhaps if I had been given the opportunity to experience that discomfort when I was a teenager, it wouldn't have taken so many years for me to understand Mary's isolation or John Wallace's objections to *Huckleberry Finn*.

By no means am I saying that I agree with Mr. Wallace's point of view. Freedom, identity, and dignity are universal human concerns. Mark Twain may show us the ignorance and hypocrisy of a society which places one man above another because of race, but he also shows us the nobility of the individual who transcends that ignorance. *The Adventures of Huckleberry Finn* challenges us to examine the foibles of our society as well as the prejudices and factitiousness in our own lives.

While I do not agree with Mr. Wallace, I do know that we cannot fully understand our own position on a controversial issue without examining it in relation to opposing views. If we expect our students to function as thinking human beings, we cannot protect them from controversy. We must not only allow the free exchange of divergent ideas, but also encourage it, even when those ideas do not concur with our own and even when those ideas make us "uncomfortable." Of course, we should be sensitive to the feelings of others, but we must not shrink from confrontation, for it is only through confrontation with our own beliefs and those of others that we learn to see our world in its totality.

ENDNOTES

1. Edwin McDowell, New York Times News Service, "Letter Shows Twain Helped Black Student," *The Ledger Star*, Norfolk, VA, March 14, 1985, p. 1.

2. Editorial, "Expelling Huck Finn," *The Ledger Star,* Norfolk, VA, April 11, 1982, p. 2.

3. Editorial, *"Adventures of Huckleberry Finn* to Remain in Curriculum," *The Ledger Star,* Norfolk, VA, April 13, 1982, p.2.

4. Editorial, "Expelling Huck Finn."

5. Edward Ziegler, "Huck Finn at 100," *Reader's Digest,* 126(February 1985), p. 99.

Linda Bulman, Green Run High School, Virginia Beach, Virginia

CREATING AN INDIVIDUAL AND CLASS DEFINITION OF "COURAGE"

While my students are reading the early chapters of *The Red Badge of Courage,* I ask them to spend one day discussing and refining what they mean when they talk about "courage." Each student does a rank ordering of ten events, either historical or current, which have been considered courageous by some and foolish, pointless, or insane by others. I distribute the following directions:

Directions: Read each of the following examples of courage; then rank order them 1–10, 1 being the most impressive act of courage, 10 the least impressive. Be prepared to defend your choice. Having used this process as a warm-up, write your own definition of courage in the space provided.

1. A parent runs back into a burning house to save the baby.
2. A man deliberately drives a truck carrying explosives into a Marine barracks and blows it and himself up.
3. A Greek soldier runs 26 miles from the battlefield to Athens, then dies from exhaustion after reporting the news of victory.
4. A father with arthritis works 20 years in a steel mill to save money for his son's college education.
5. A Japanese man with a parachute on his back skis down Mt. Everest. He is the first to ever attempt it.
6. A mother whose daughter is killed by a drunk driver organizes M.A.D.D.; she petitions state and federal governments to get tough with new D.W.I. legislation.
7. In the midst of a fierce Vietnam battle, a soldier wipes out a machine-gun nest single-handedly, then dives on a live grenade to save his buddies.
8. Although white students taunt her mercilessly, a 15-year-old girl is the first black to attend Little Rock Central High in the 1950s.
9. An off-duty policeman shoots and kills brutal thieves attempting to rob a 7-11 store.
10. A scientist gives up friends and family (his wife leaves him; his children don't know him) to discover a cure for a dreaded disease.

My definition of courage:

Students talk about their differing points of view in small groups and then summarize their discussions for the entire class. Gleaning ideas from each group, I write a general definition of "courage" on the board to be used later as a standard for evaluating the behavior of Henry Fleming. I find that this supplementary activity adds clarity to later discussions of Henry's actions. It helps students to deal with the issue of whether or not Henry, through the experience of combat, has truly achieved manhood or heroism, or whether he is merely demonstrating a primal instinct for survival or violence.

I encourage students to bring in their own examples of events that fit this description. The best examples may either be discussed as a class or added to the list that students receive for rank ordering.

James Motzko, Hopkins High School, Minnetonka, Minnesota

THE RED BADGE OF COURAGE

*We never know how high we are
Till we are called to rise.*

Emily Dickinson's words express that yearning, so strong in youth, to test oneself. *The Red Badge of Courage* speaks to that yearning, just one of the reasons for selecting this classic for study. But there are more. The novel attracts students because it dramatizes breaking away from home. It shows youth's resentment toward and need for authority. It tells how one can be alone in the company of many. It reveals human weaknesses like pride and cowardice as it shows our potential for heroism. It depicts fear of failure and yet is a success story of sorts.

Teachers too have reasons for selecting *Red Badge*. The novel provides an opportunity to examine closely certain elements of fiction, especially style, multiple themes, character development, and the relationship between mood and setting. Crane's work also serves as an introduction to the psychological novel and has, in fact, been read by many as a psychological study of fear. The book allows students to discover truths about themselves and others and about life. Finally, the book is short, and schedules sometimes preclude the consideration of longer works.

PRELIMINARY SMALL-GROUP ACTIVITIES

Divide the class into groups of four or five students and assign the following tasks. Each group later reports to the class on the results of its exploration, and the class responds with questions and comments.

1. Trace the events of the novel in sequence; note the time span of the novel as a whole.
2. Trace the steps in Henry's development from youth to man. How does his changing view of war reflect this maturation.
3. Record and categorize color images.
4. Identify figures of speech (metaphor, simile, personification) and group them into such categories as nature, machine, animal, religious, and so on.
5. Jot down typical examples of language used by the narrator, by Henry, and by other characters. What conclusions can be drawn?
6. Select several passages from the novel and list the verbs, adjectives, and nouns. Examine these lists. Do patterns emerge? What observations can you make?

CLASS DISCUSSION

Although class editions of *Red Badge* usually contain helpful discussion questions and teachers have lists of their own, here are a few of the questions I regularly use. Insist that students cite evidence from the text to support their answers.

General Questions

1. What is the significance of the title? What does *red* symbolize? *Badge?* How is Henry's red badge ironic? What is the meaning of

courage? Are there different kinds of courage? Are courageous actions similar to/different from *brave, heroic, intrepid* ones? Are there circumstances under which a person might be more courageous than at other times? In a war or other disaster, are those who remain at home cowardly?

2. What is the effect of Crane's use of the general rather than the specific in character and place names and in time?

3. What statement about the relationship between man and nature does the novel make? You might consider images of fog, rain, and sun as a beginning.

4. In what ways are the novel and its protagonist affected by the fact that except for chapter one no women are included? Would a writer today exclude women in a war novel?

Questions That Focus on the Protagonist

1. Why does Crane choose a fatherless youth as his protagonist?

2. What are the youth's feelings about the enemy? Toward the officers? How do the officers feel/act toward their men?

3. Was Henry right in chapter one that "whatever he had learned of himself was here of no avail"? What does he discover about his physical self? Moral self? Social self? Is he disappointed or pleased with what he finds?

4. Itemize in specific terms what Henry learns from others and from each experience in battle.

5. At what times does Henry become "not a man but a member"? Can you recall times when you experienced this feeling? Did you think and act in the same way as you would have thought and acted as an individual?

6. Trace the parallels between the fighting and Henry's journey into "self." When does Henry talk banalities? When is he most pretentious? When does he seem to be rationalizing? Would Henry's maturing process have occurred so rapidly if he had remained at home?

7. Was Henry a hero or a coward?

Questions That Focus on the War

1. What factual information about this battle, this war, does the reader learn?

2. How does a civil war differ from a war against other nations?
3. Discuss Crane's image of war as "the blood-swollen god." Can you apply this idea to times other than war?
4. How does Crane differentiate between the popular view of war and the personal or private view?

LIBRARY PROJECTS

These topics may be investigated by individuals or small groups. The results may be presented in writing, as panels and speeches, or as bulletin board displays.

1. Report on—or demonstrate—recent findings about how colors affect human beings. Can you apply these findings to Crane's use of color?
2. Build a case for *each* of the following: *The Red Badge of Courage* is an example of naturalism, realism, romanticism, impressionism, all of the above, none of the above.
3. Investigate the life of Stephen Crane and find out about some of his other works. "The Open Boat," "The Blue Hotel," and "The Bride Comes to Yellow Sky" are good possibilities if you're interested in short stories. You might also like to look at some of the poems in the collection *War Is Kind*.
4. Analyze Lincoln's Gettysburg address. Discuss its content, form, purpose, and style in relation to *Red Badge*.
5. Find out about impressionistic painting and music. Bring in examples to share with the class. Be prepared to lead a discussion of their relationship to each other and to Crane's style.
6. Read or reread William Golding's *Lord of the Flies*. What comparisons can you make with the corpse scene at the end of chapter seven of *Red Badge?* Are there other similarities between the two novels?
7. Read another Civil War novel. Compare it to *Red Badge* and draw conclusions. Possibilities include MacKinley Kantor's *Andersonville*, Margaret Mitchell's *Gone with the Wind*, Irene Hunt's *Across Five Aprils*.
8. Analyze war posters. Recruitment posters are an interesting possibility. Report to the class on your conclusions.

WRITING ASSIGNMENTS

1. Recall a time when you felt overpowering fear. Explain the circumstances. Analyze your reasons for fear. Describe the physical and emotional effects of that fear. What happened? Were your fears realized? Were you pleased with how you acted? Were you changed in any way by this experience?

2. Using *Red Badge* as a point of reference, consider the passage of time, how it can stand still or rush past. Include examples of this phenomenon from *Red Badge,* from other works you've read, and from personal experience. Draw a conclusion about the nature of time.

3. Describe Henry's mixed feelings in leaving home and mother. How does his mother feel? Why does she mention socks several times? Extend your observations to include similar experiences and reactions that apply to most young people and their parents.

4. Imagine that you are Henry. The battle has ended. Write a letter to your mother, a letter to a friend who stayed home, and a letter to the "dark girl."

5. Using Stephen Crane as your writing model, create a scene of your own for *Red Badge.*

6. Write a news report of the battle. Then write an editorial and a human interest story. You may add details of your own invention.

7. Adapt *one* of the preliminary small group activities, class discussion questions, or library research projects as the subject for an essay. After you have done some preliminary thinking, discuss your choice with your teacher.

FOLLOW-UP SMALL GROUP ACTIVITIES

1. Prepare a reading of one or more passages from the novel. Be attentive to the sounds and rhythms of language and how these elements enhance images called forth by the words.

2. Dramatize (or pantomime) a scene from the novel. Use props and/or background music if you wish.

3. Compose and perform for the class a folk song or a dance that relates to the events of or a scene from the novel.

4. Represent the novel through a watercolor, drawing, collage, or poster.

5. Relate the novel to contemporary times through an editorial

cartoon or a comic strip.

6. You are the director in charge of filming the novel. How will you cast it? How will you handle the camera? What do you have in mind for setting and sound? Will you make symbolic use of color? How?

7. Assemble a slide/tape presentation that depicts a theme from the novel. You might consider presenting that theme in contemporary terms.

8. Interview several people from different age groups who have served in wars. Think carefully about the questions you will ask. Support your findings and conclusions in writing or as a panel discussion.

Beverly Haley, The Language Works, Fort Morgan, Colorado

THINKING THROUGH DILEMMAS

What a splendid idea Sartre had in *Nausea*. Remember the character Roquentin? His mind seems to split in half, which gives him the ability to run through the streets of Bouville feeling the cobblestones under his feet while he writes down the experience as it occurs. Sartre captivates us with this technique. We are drawn to this evocative sense of simultaneity, of experiencing and recording an experience. I'm left with a dilemma when I think about the incongruity.

How can the mind adjust to these very separate dimensions working as one? Yet that is exactly what occurs. The notion certainly stimulates my thinking.

I want to understand how Sartre led me to believe that his character could act, react, interpret, and record experiences simultaneously. I believe we have this power--sometimes. I started to think about ways to tap such potential in classroom activities.

I redesigned a unit in my literature and composition class for high school seniors after I thought about Roquentin and his multidimensional antics. The old unit centered on a study of Henry James's *Turn of the Screw* (W. W. Norton, 1966). We probed the mystery and then focused on critical interpretation of this short novel. Yes, we had some personalized interaction with the text, as Louise Rosenblatt would suggest. The culminating assignment was an interpretive essay.

In the new unit, activities build an awareness of how we think--the acrobatics and fluidity, the leaps of imagination, the grueling task of evaluation, the experiencing and recording and interpreting. Gymnastics of the mind, I'd venture to say.

INITIAL WRITING AND CATALOGING OF DILEMMAS

After we read *The Turn of the Screw* (many other novels or short stories would work equally well), exploration begins with three impromptu writing topics: "Are the ghosts real?" "Is the governess sane or insane?" "Are the children guilty or innocent?" Writing serves as a tool for discovery at this point. Each question encourages students to think through the complexity of dilemmas introduced in the story. After fifteen or twenty minutes of writing time, students have a better grasp of the deliberate ambiguity and mystery, the uncertainties that carry no easy resolutions.

Stretch student imagination and thinking by following the impromptu writing topics with an oral cataloging of dilemmas in *The Turn of the Screw*. Students often begin with the governess, looking at her confrontations with the children, the ghosts, or herself. Then students move to less obvious confrontations: the uncle's lack of concern, the naïveté of Mrs. Grose, the letter from Miles's school. I record dilemmas on the board as students present them. Tapping the powers of the right brain, I end the cataloging with a visual demonstration as I prod for a kernel dilemma (e.g., knowledge versus innocence, good versus evil, imagination versus fact). Once we have established a core dilemma, I diagram, using concentric circles and connecting lines, the spiderweb of interrelated dilemmas present in James's story. With little prompting, students take the lead in this visual pursuit, seeking the interrelatedness of conflicting forces.

Students challenge themselves to add circles by constantly moving into subtle realms, building circles based on setting, on character action or lack of action, on the appearance of outside forces, on silence, and on extenuating circumstances. They speculate freely when pressed to add another layer. Structural dilemmas, such as the half-frame where a love-struck Douglas begins a story but disappears, never resurfacing, or the use of a manuscript rather than a narrator, provide students with new levels of understanding. Hidden dilemmas, the power of one dilemma to enhance another, and the root or related roots of key dilemmas all add new connections. Students build a visual diagram, a record of their journey through James's story, showing relationships with lines, stars, and arrows. I find that this visual record of thinking brings power and sureness to the students' imaginative quest.

RESOLVING A DILEMMA BY ORAL COMPOSITION

Next I ask students to consider possible resolutions not given in the story. There is one wrinkle in the speculation—solutions cannot detract from the meaning or mystery of the story. "That is a tough proposition," students tell me. As students consider this next "turn" in our study of James's novel, I remind them that James tells us "the story won't tell" (3). Exactly. Our new dilemma, one we will work with for the next several days, has been introduced.

I ask students to write an imaginative and speculative addition to the work that will solve one of the story's dilemmas before it happens, during a pivotal incident, or after the fact. As students create this new piece, they tap their own understanding of James's style, pace, and point of view. They engage in imaginative thinking when they consider possible additions, rearrangements, and deletions dependent on existing actions, characters, and events. Students fit their creative piece into the story line, matching the style so that a reader might not suspect a breaking point in the original. Some suggested topics include creating a dream sequence for one or more characters, writing a diary entry or a letter that reveals information, having a character make a discovery during the story, writing an end frame, and giving new action or speech to a character (e.g., a silent character might be given a voice). I know of no better way to have students exercise their imaginations while studying literature. In theory and practice, students discover new ways of thinking about James's novel.

I throw a final "turn" into this unit. Remembering the divided mind of Roquentin, I ask students to write their additions to *The Turn of the Screw* in an atypical way. Students are to do their initial drafting and related brain work *orally*. Most of us carry on internal verbalizations as we write, but the audience for these dialogues is ourselves. In this activity, the writer will have an external audience for this verbal composing.

The students form pairs. One partner is the writer for the next two days; the other is the eavesdropper and interpreter of the writing process. The writers are given a general way of solving a dilemma present in the story. For example, students might solve a dilemma by creating a new character whose arrival interferes with or changes an outcome, or students might change an action or reaction of any one character. I have several options in mind and use different alternatives for each member of the pair. Eavesdroppers in the first round tend to jump ahead and start working on the assignment if they know the topics will be the same for them, and thus they lose the benefit of spontaneous oral composing. Once writers have a clear idea of the options I give the following instructions:

> Compose out loud. Say everything that comes into your mind. Get the workings of your mind floating in the air in front of you. Verbalize all of your thoughts. Write down what you normally would write once you have orally sifted the chaff from the grain.

This is a good time to talk with students about the critical part of the writing mind. Remind students how much time they spend mentally editing and critiquing before they put words on paper. Remind them of the opposite experience where "fast writes" or "brain writes" lead them into the creative part of their writing minds.

The listeners need instructions also. This group eavesdrops on the writers' oral thinking. While the writers say everything that comes to mind and then write down what they want in their first drafts, the listeners make notes. They observe the writers' thoughts, watch the writers' habits while composing, and interpret the type of thinking they observe. Listeners might consider how much time writers follow creative bursts, how much time writers spend judging and critiquing their thoughts. How much time at speculation? At evaluation? In a real sense, eavesdroppers provide a link between thought and the written product. Listeners should not interfere or interject comments. They serve as recorders of the composing process.

This exercise magnifies the working of the writer's mind, exploring and interpreting the unconscious processes of composing. It will help the student pairs develop sensitivity to the thinking that takes place during writing. One student recorded his partner Stacy's oral thoughts in this way:

I'm intrigued by the uncle's silence in the novel and wonder if I can bring him into the story without ruining the atmosphere where the governess must function alone. I want to give her strength enough to control the situation . . . I must find a place where his intrusion would seem natural . . . Where are the places that might work? The uncle could bring Miles home from school; he could escort the governess to Bly and see Quent himself . . . no, all are too obvious. One of the children could write for help . . . might be the best of all . . . Uncle resolves not to go or aid . . . one place to start this strand would be at the end of chapter XV. Start the hint where James writes ". . . He marched off alone into church." I'll add "and he later proved full wit at trying to get his uncle's attention, but of that I will arrive all too soon."

Stacy has begun with a thread of imaginative writing that will blend through several chapters. Her observer goes on to interpret her brain writing:

Stacy is a cautious creator. She is careful in preparing: she scans sections of the book, pauses, looks at circumstances from many angles. When a thought strikes her, she talks it out. She says it aloud to try it on for size. Once she has verbalized ideas, she writes at a hurried pace. Then when the spurt of writing is finished, she slacks off on her pace, studies the passage and begins her search again.

Stacy reflects on her own experience:

In the past two days, I learned something about myself as a writer. I see more of the process I go through. I feel as if I have been honest with myself. I know that I am stubborn in writing, that I need to be more flexible, to allow myself to move on when I'm stumped on a word or idea. It helps to bring my methods in the open where I can try to take advantage of my best patterns of thought. I started thinking about the critical/creative parts of my mind. I'll try new strategies each time I write.

The exercise is designed to make the unconscious conscious and the internal external. After two days, the listeners discuss their reactions to the writers' mental flurries. The pairs switch roles for the next two days, receive new topics, and repeat the process. The actual writing of the imaginative section of the novel is ongoing, as students rework and refine their final compositions.

Such oral activity reproduces mental language and explores writers' thinking minds. I believe this assignment alters students' sensitivity to their thought processes. In a sense, these young writers experience conversations with themselves. They have a record of the workings of their imaginative and critical minds, the many chance associations, the give-and-take as ideas develop. The sequence of logical thinking and mental leaps provides students with the footprints of thought that help carry these writers through the streets of their own Bouville. Through the assignment, they develop better understanding of themselves as writers and the writing process. My goal is to create increasingly fluent improvisers, fleet of foot and mind like Roquentin.

Ruth Vinz, Boise High School, Boise, Idaho

7 EMPHASIS: MODERN AMERICAN NOVELS

DEMYSTIFYING SHERWOOD ANDERSON'S *WINESBURG, OHIO*

There seems to be something mystical about writers. With words as their only tools they are able to create visionary worlds. As readers, we often enter these splendid worlds without being aware that the act of creation can be as fascinating to study as the literary work itself. Indeed, the understanding of a writer's creative endeavors provides a natural entry into the study of literature.

In our classrooms, we approach literature through writing as an excellent motivator of students. Students gain a unique appreciation for a work of literature by encountering a series of writing decisions that parallel those faced by experienced authors. By writing before they read, students come to understand the dilemmas that plot, characterization, narration, and theme present. Ultimately, students discover that writing is not a mysterious process but a series of calculated risks which they are capable of mastering.

Below is an outline of suggested prereading activities that we employ with Sherwood Anderson's *Winesburg, Ohio*. These activities attempt to help students to understand the book and encourage them to read the material more closely. These assignments may be altered or deleted according to circumstances, time, or personal teaching objectives.

Assignment 1:

This study of *Winesburg, Ohio* begins with a prewriting exercise which introduces the setting of the book to students. Since many of our students have not lived in a small town, we want to help them to envision the details and to determine the effects of such a setting on the story. Our first activity draws from the students' resources but also requires research, both formal and informal.

Students begin this activity by exchanging their conceptions of small towns. They brainstorm the physical layout of small towns that they have seen or lived in, including street plans, parks, schools, businesses, town halls, etc. In addition to the physical layout, students need to list the possible occupations of people who live in small towns. For example, there may be a mayor, sheriff, or general store owner. Near the end of this discussion, students prepare a final list of small town characteristics and record them in their notes.

In the next step, students are asked to move from stereotypical information to creating a unique small town. It is their responsibility as a class to decide the geographical location for the town and to research the area so that the details are authentic. It will probably require a vote on the part of the entire class to decide the exact spot. We have found it best that the location be fictitious because students understand the factors inherent in designing a successful town when they experience the growth process themselves. Several days are allotted for researching the chosen area for its history, geographical features, and natural resources.

After students gather and exchange all necessary information, they vote on suggested names for their town and actual population size. The class then divides into groups, and each group creates a topographical map of the town, taking into account physical features derived from information they have already gathered.

Approximately one week later, these maps are exhibited to the entire class. The class votes on the best one, which then serves as the model for the following assignments. All groups receive credit for their work.

Assignment 2:
Once the setting of the town has been decided, it is time for each student to become a character within the town. The best way to start is to list plausible professions that might be found in this setting. Students are to select one profession or job without duplication in order to ensure variety of character.

Once the professions are decided (yes, there may be arguing and the need to flip a coin!) students are asked to write thumbnail biographical sketches of their characters. These sketches might include name, physical features, marital status, hobbies, and possible eccentricities. These sketches are then photocopied and distributed to the class. Using these sketches as a basis, students will take one day to introduce their characters to one another and to establish the relationships and bonds that one might expect in community living.

Assignment 3:

The Small Town Dossier is an assignment that further develops characterization. Students need to decide what documents help to establish an individual's identity. The first response is usually "a driver's license," but with additional prompting, students are able to create a long list of such documents. For example, students might list a marriage license, a last will and testament, school records, dental records, charge accounts, insurance policies, and professional affiliations.

After students have adequately developed this list, their next task is to design an identification folder for their fictional characters. Students may be paired for this assignment so that they can share resources and thereby develop more authentic documents. Students often show a great deal of ingenuity in this step. For example, one of our students, the daughter of a personnel director, included sample personnel forms and job application blanks in her character's dossier. Other students have had identification bracelets and dog tags engraved with their characters' names. The entire packet for each character should contain at least ten items, enabling students to develop a certain level of complexity for their characters.

Assignment 4:

Although a character may be well known through his or her dossier, the environment can serve to further distinguish this character from all others. For this assignment, students describe the room, office, or store in which their character spends most of his or her time. The description does not have to be longer than a paragraph, but it should be filled with details that provide insight into the character's true personality.

This assignment works best when the character describes this "place" through his or her own eyes. The topic sentence, therefore, should include the personal pronoun "I"; the name of the room, office, or store being described; and the character's feelings about this place. For example, if a student's character is a traveling salesperson, the opening sentence might read: "I cannot recall a time when I entered a buyer's office that a feeling of anxiety did not overcome me." From this point, the rest of the paragraph should describe the objects in that room which logically echo this feeling of desolation. Students may need to do a little research to come up with accurate details. By writing this descriptive paragraph, students begin to understand the emotional makeup of their fictional character.

Assignment 5:

Students are now asked to read excerpts from Studs Terkel's book *Working*. In this nonfiction work, Terkel interviews individuals from all sectors of the working world, allowing them to tell their own stories. For this assignment, students take on the persona of their fictional character and tell the character's story. Students must determine proper diction for their character, remaining consistent throughout the piece. Students easily understand this format and enjoy writing in the first-person narrative style. The intent of this assignment is to reveal the character's perception of himself/herself and life.

Assignment 6:

At this point, *Winesburg, Ohio* can be assigned to the class. We spent several class periods reviewing and discussing questions generated by the writing thus far, such as these:

1. Has the author created a realistic small town setting?
2. Do the characters' surroundings complement their personalities?
3. Are the characters' actions consistent with their personality traits?
4. Are the traits of each character fully developed?
5. How well does the author know his characters?

Assignment 7:

Early in the discussion that takes place in Assignment 6, students generally begin to realize that Anderson made a stylistic decision before he wrote this novel. He chose to develop a major character in each chapter; thus, his entire novel is really a series of character sketches. Each sketch is told through the eyes of the narrator, George. Because of this decision, much of the expected interaction between characters is eliminated.

In order for students to better understand this writing decision, we ask them to form groups of three to five to write a story which features their fictional characters in a strong conflict with each other. The emphasis should be on the action or plot. These stories are then read to the class as the basis for debating whether a writer gains or loses readers by emphasizing character analysis over plot. Students may need several days for this assignment.

Assignment 8:

For this last writing assignment, students take on the personality of George, the narrator of *Winesburg, Ohio*. Through the eyes of this persona, they write their own chapter of the novel, revealing a significant flaw in their character's makeup. As George, they then must analyze this flaw and state its relevance to his (or their) life. Although George's recognition of this human flaw should not significantly alter his life, the reader should sense that George grows in maturity.

This unit on *Winesburg, Ohio* may be used as a springboard for teaching other similar works such as *Dandelion Wine, Something Wicked This Way Comes,* or *To Kill a Mockingbird.* All of these works of literature include small town settings, characters who possess personality flaws, and narrators who mature by reacting to the events around them.

Andrea L. Watson, Rocky Mountain Hebrew Academy, Denver, Colorado; Linda Arnold, Heritage High School, Littleton, Colorado; and Madelyn Braverman, George Washington High School, Denver, Colorado

F. SCOTT FITZGERALD'S *THE GREAT GATSBY*

Fast cars, wild parties, shady business dealings . . . . These are a few of the intriguing elements found in F. Scott Fitzgerald's *The Great Gatsby*—a novel that invites its readers to enter the Jazz Age. Studying *The Great Gatsby* promotes discussion of values; the glittering world of the Roaring Twenties appeals to students, yet at the same time they are able to detect the artificiality and moral bankruptcy of the society Fitzgerald depicts. Obtain if you can the film version of *The Great Gatsby* starring Robert Redford and Mia Farrow; it paints a memorable portrait of the excessive opulence of Gatsby's world.

In addition to presenting provocative subject matter, *The Great Gatsby* teaches important stylistic lessons. Through Nick Carraway, it provides an excellent example of a first-person retrospective point of view. Students can learn the technical demands an author faces in using a central intelligence. They can also learn how effective this point of view is for charting the growth in the insight of a narrating character. A second stylistic feature is the use of a complex chronology, one that shifts back and forth between the present and the past. This type of chronology provides a complete picture of the protagonist only at the end of the work, and is typical of modern literature. Yet a third lesson stems from the use of imagery clusters. Because of the brevity of the novel, students can easily trace the patterns of images that Fitzgerald emphasizes.

CLASS DISCUSSION

There's nothing like a good discussion question to inspire creative dispute among members of the class. Here are questions that you can use along with your own favorites, either during the course of reading the novel or after everyone in the class has finished reading.

1. What is the significance of the title *The Great Gatsby?* Is Jay Gatsby truly great? Explain your answer.
2. How is marriage depicted in the novel? How successful is the marriage between Daisy and Tom Buchanan? And that between Myrtle and George Wilson?
3. What is Gatsby's dream? Does he ever see Daisy as she really is?
4. Compare Jay Gatsby to James Gatz. What does Fitzgerald mean when he writes that "Jay Gatsby of West Egg, Long Island, sprang from his Platonic conception of himself"?
5. How does Fitzgerald reveal that Gatsby is an isolated character?
6. What does the novel say about materialism? What, if any, are the similarities between the 1920s and the 1980s?
7. How does Fitzgerald relate Gatsby's dream to the American Dream? What seems to be his message about the American Dream as expressed in the last two paragraphs of the novel?

WRITING ASSIGNMENTS

As a follow-up to reading and discussion, suggest one of the writing assignments listed below.

1. Look up the word *hedonism* in the dictionary and write a short essay revealing how the concept applies to Fitzgerald's novel.
2. Compose a paragraph on each of the following items, explaining how each reflects Gatsby's tastes and lifestyle:

   a. his house
   b. his car
   c. his parties
   d. his guest list (given in Chapter IV)

3. Pretend that you are Nick Carraway and write two journal entries, one giving your impression of Jay Gatsby upon first meeting him and the other giving your final assessment of the man after you've returned to the Midwest.
4. Compare Tom Buchanan's relationship with his wife, Daisy, to his relationship with Myrtle Wilson. What does he want from each woman? Does he love either of them?
5. Some critics suggest that although Gatsby is the principal figure in the action of the novel, Nick is the most significant character. Discuss the novel as a record of Nick's moral development. What does Nick learn from his experiences in the East?

SMALL-GROUP ACTIVITIES

Here are some additional ideas you might try when teaching *The Great Gatsby*.

1. Divide the class into research teams and ask them to provide the class with information about the Roaring Twenties. Give each group a list of one or more questions such as the following:

   a. What was the political climate of the United States during the decade? Who were the country's major political leaders? How did people respond to the aftermath of World War I?
   b. What was the economic status of the United States? Was the decade a time of growth or recession? Explain why.
   c. What was Prohibition and how did it affect the nation?
   d. What was the status of women at this time? What changes were occurring in the institution of marriage and in young people's moral standards?

e. What types of music were popular? What subjects were mentioned in popular song lyrics? Do you think that young people in the 1920s listened to popular music for the same reasons that young people today do? If so, what are those reasons?

2. Assign one major character—Jay Gatsby, Nick Carraway, Daisy Buchanan, Tom Buchanan, and Jordan Baker—to each of five groups. Ask each group to decide upon three adjectives that best describe the character and to be able to explain the reasons for selecting these words. Have each group select one passage from the novel that seems to reflect the character's personality well.

3. Form teams of students to examine the imagery in the novel. Each team must search for one particular set of images that recur throughout the novel. Among the possibilities are the following images:

   a. color (especially green)
   b. eyes or vision (whether accurate or distorted)
   c. a wasteland (a barren landscape, ashes, dust)
   d. cars
   e. time
   f. death

4. Appoint a group of students to trace the novel's chronology. The group should consider the following questions: In what season does the book begin? In what season does Nick first go east? In what season does Gatsby die? In what chapter or chapters do we learn of Gatsby's boyhood? Of his adolescence? Of his early relationship with Daisy? Of his war experiences? Of his business dealings?

5. Divide the class into three groups and assign each group to prepare a brief talk, based on passages from the book, on one of the following topics:

   a. Nick's role *as narrator*, including where he is when he is writing the book, what his attitude toward Jay Gatsby is, and how he solves the problem of presenting information that he did not witness.
   b. Nick *as a man* who gets caught up in the corrupt world of the East. Decide if and when Nick seems not to act according to

his moral standards.

   c.   Nick *as a detached character*. In what ways is he involved in the action and in what ways is he separate from it?

Lynn P. Shackelford, Greenville, South Carolina

THE GRAPES OF WRATH

In January of 1939 John Steinbeck was exhausted—and fearful. Worn by what he called "thousands of hours" of research and writing, he spent two weeks in bed worrying about his latest completed manuscript.

Steinbeck was both wrong and right to worry. *The Grapes of Wrath* swept the best-seller lists of those last years of the Great Depression partly because of its appeal as a historical novel. But its popularity was and is tied to controversy; for nearly fifty years it has been attacked for its use of language, for its realism, and for its politics.

English teachers know the hazards of teaching *The Grapes of Wrath*—the controversies, the length, the reading ability and maturity of their students. They also know that Steinbeck won a Nobel Prize and that his novel won a Pulitzer Prize; they know that the book is included in the list of classics that the National Endowment for the Humanities believes high school students should read. And they know that careful reading and discussion, especially in a classroom of mature juniors and seniors, are important in understanding controversial classics.

Plan to spend at least seventeen days with this many-faceted novel.

Suggested Schedule

Days 1–3	Introduction to the novel, including a discussion of Steinbeck and the Okies, the geography of the book, and time for reading
Day 4	Explaining and assigning the position paper
Days 5–7	Reading and reviewing events of the Great Depression
Days 8–10	Discussing the Steinbeck style and "phalanx theory" through supplementary reading; reading the novel
Day 11	Discussing Steinbeck and the Nobel and Pulitzer prizes
Days 12–14	Prewriting, drafting, anecdotal research; reading the novel
Days 15–16	Films: *The Great American Novel:* The Grapes of Wrath (Columbia Broadcasting System, 1967) and *The Grapes of Wrath* (Fox, 1940)
Day 17	Paper due with time for in-class proofreading

The first three days should provide background for the novel as well as time for reading. Remind students that Steinbeck began his research on migrants in 1936, when he wrote a series of articles for the San Francisco *News,* an exposé of California workers who came primarily from Oklahoma and Arkansas. Then in 1937 he toured the Oklahoma Dust Bowl and in 1938 visited migrant camps in California.

Refer to the dedication: Carol is Steinbeck's wife, who both typed the novel and suggested its title—a Civil War song. Remind students that this was a highly controversial book that offended both Californians and Oklahomans, who thought it was a slanted, ugly picture of their states. Then define the basic plot—the Joad family move from the Dust Bowl of Oklahoma—using a map of the United States. (There are maps of both Steinbeck's California and the Joads's trek in my *Writing Seminars in the Content Areas: In Search of Hemingway, Salinger, and Steinbeck,* published by NCTE.) Finally, point to Steinbeck's use of interchapters that divide the plot and convey his anger, philosophy, and compassion for the Okies. Perhaps one interchapter should be read aloud.

The assignment on Day 4 is crucial to the success of the entire project. Students are asked to begin work on a three- to five-page position paper in which they limit their analysis of the novel to a single focus. This position is to be organized, supported by concrete detail, and mechanically sound. Here are some of the position suggestions I offer, which students are free to accept, reject, or adapt.

1. What is the meaning of "family" in this book?
2. One critic said: The book is a "story of the awakening of a man's conscience." Is it? Whose conscience?
3. Is this book an attack on America? Is Steinbeck advocating socialism? Is the government camp a symbol?
4. What is the meaning of the land? Remember that the land, the American "good earth," was so important to Americans in 1939—and now.
5. Discuss the ending—so vivid and controversial.
6. Answer those critics who want to ban this book from high schools.

By Day 5 students should have read a good chunk of the novel. Now is the time to place the artifact in its historical setting. Using the chalkboard, develop a 1930s chronology: begin with the 1929 stock market crash, move through FDR's New Deal pledge in 1932 and his 100 days of 1933, from the 1935 Dust Bowl and the 1937 migration, to the beginning of World War II in 1939. Days 6 and 7 can give reinforcement with films like *Life in the Thirties* (NBC, 1959); filmstrips like *Grapes of Wrath and the 1930s*; records like Woody Guthrie's *Dust Bowl Blues*; or books like Studs Terkel's *Hard Times* oral histories (Washington Square Press, 1978). (Also: with student assistance, develop a bulletin board and a class library with 1930s artifacts and good photographic materials, such as the Time-Life *Fabulous Century* volumes.) Here may be the time to use community people who remember the 1930s.

Days 8 to 10 are a crucial time. Students are deep into the novel. Now is a time to reflect on Steinbeck's style and mind and to return to the idea of a position paper. Instead of reading from *The Grapes of Wrath*, I select one of the following stories to read aloud: "The Harness," "The Snake," or "Breakfast." Through discussion we piece together the Steinbeck who was sensitive to nature, who believed himself to be "a scientist of the imagination." Ask students: "If you had to write a paper on this story, what would be your position?" We go on to consider how we might document and organize that position based on the story we just read. On Day 10, I add theory, Steinbeck's (and that of his friend Ed Ricketts—The Doc in "The Snake") concept of the "phalanx": groups are separate and distinct from the individuals that compose them, yet the groups have transcendent power because people often behave on the basis of the group nature. Thus the Joads's movement westward is a phalanx, as is the movement of the Okies. The Californians, who as a group oppose the Okies but may relent as individuals, form a phalanx. Some observers note that the turtle of the novel is also a tortoise or *testudo*, the same word for the ancient Roman phalanx—a close order of advancing soldiers with shields locked overhead.

Day 11 honors Steinbeck's receipt of the Pulitzer Prize in 1940, which was instrumental in his winning of the 1962 Nobel Prize. You may wish to refer to W.J. Stuckey's *The Pulitzer Prize Novels* (University of Oklahoma Press) and to *American Winners of the Nobel Literary Prize*, edited by Warren G. French and Walter E. Kidd (University Microfilms International). This is a good time to discuss awards and prizes that both delight and frighten authors. While the Swedish Academy called Steinbeck a "bold observer of human behavior," the author was always shy and fearful of prizes—especially the Nobel, which he felt was the kiss of death.

By Day 12 the students should be nearly finished reading the novel. Now we spend time talking about how we write, how we get ideas. Students also share the positions that they are developing in their papers.

Days 13 and 14 deal with an important decision: Who is this man, John Steinbeck? I ask students to do some simple research about the man behind the book. For this purpose I assemble in the classroom as much Steinbeck material as I can from public, school, and personal libraries, from friends and colleagues and students, from old textbooks—his collected letters, biographies, newspaper and magazine clippings, the recording of him reading "Johnny Bear," posters and pictures. Each student finds an anecdote to share with the class. On Day 14 students tell stories about Steinbeck's lifelong interest in King Arthur, his love of dogs, his college pranks, his wonderful letters, his red pony, his relationship with his wives and sons.

The book is read. The prewriting, drafting, and documenting are nearly over. Perhaps now is the time for a final visual statement. On Days 15 and 16 I have used John Ford's 1940 *Grapes of Wrath* (now available in videotape), which Steinbeck called "hard, truthful." Or the educational film *The Great American Novel: The Grapes of Wrath* can offer twenty-five minutes of thoughtful parallels between 1930s Okies and modern migrants.

On Day 17, with time for in-class proofreading, the position papers are collected. (Some instructors may prefer to collect them before the film, then grade and return them on Day 17.) While the position paper could end the unit, let me suggest an alternative: Select three or four papers to be shared with the class the following day. Have the writers read their papers aloud, and let the class determine the position of each paper and comment on the clarity and support of each.

After these seventeen days, *The Grapes of Wrath* is no longer just a title. It is, as one of my students said, "an achievement." Through a logical progression, this classic has been discovered: its complex plot and its tie to history, its author and his lyrical passion to arouse humankind, its enduring popularity and its controversial nature. Through reading and writing and discussion, the book has come alive. Perhaps some readers' nerves have been tested, and perhaps some are still not satisfied. But all that may be the final achievement of a classic.

Brooke Workman, West High School, Iowa City, Iowa

MINOR CHARACTERS: A SECOND LOOK

Early in the term, alert literature students to watch for the not-so-obvious. Easily overlooked elements in a narrative often give added depth to understanding. A character easily slighted in the study of John Steinbeck's *Of Mice and Men* is Curley's wife. We don't even learn her name. The fact that she is the only woman in a novel populated by men, though, makes her noteworthy.

When students shift their focus from the men and analyze the character of Curley's wife, they'll gain a clearer understanding of the novel, be more aware of how seemingly small details function in other works, and reinforce what they've learned about the writer's techniques for revealing character.

As students read the novel, have them record or photocopy each passage, along with its page number, that relates to Curley's wife. Looking at all these quotations together will help reveal her character to the students. A writing assignment could then be chosen from several alternatives. Students could assume the role of Curley's wife and write a letter to her best friend, or prepare an essay showing her function in the novel, or, given guidelines from you, tell her life story in the form of an autobiography or a monologue.

When you've read the completed papers, pick several in different formats to be read aloud in class. An interesting discussion follows as students share their insights.

Add to the growing understanding of this character by reading your students the letter Steinbeck wrote to Claire Luce when she portrayed the role of Curley's wife in the Broadway production of *Of Mice and Men.* You'll find the letter in *Steinbeck: A Life in Letters,* edited by Elaine Steinbeck and Robert Wallsten (Viking Press, 1975), pp. 153–55.

Marilyn DeSalvo, Wilson High School, Youngstown, Ohio

Discussion and Writing Topics for

THE HEART IS A LONELY HUNTER

Carson McCuller's celebrated masterpiece *The Heart is a Lonely Hunter* is a novel that appeals to many readers. In a small southern town, the voiceless and the rejected struggle amidst their isolation while a young girl, Mick Kelly, earnestly pursues an intensely personal search for beauty.

Columbus, Georgia, unfolds as the background for a study of how economic, social, and political factors intrude on the personal aspirations of a drunken, bitter radical, a disillusioned black doctor, a complex restaurant owner, the adolescent, Mick Kelly, and the mute man to whom all these personalities are drawn.

In class study, the following supplemental discussion and writing topics may contribute to students' understanding of the novel's themes and characters.

Suggested Discussion Topics

1. How is Mick Kelly's coming of age explored in the novel? Which particular incidents seem to reveal the most about her initiation into the adult world? (For example, her party, her enjoyment of language study at Vo-Tech, her relationship with various members of her family.)
2. What is the significance of the dream tableau in chapter 7, part 2? How does chapter 7 relate to the novel as a whole?
3. Trace Mick's relationship with Harry and its effect on Mick.
4. How does Mick's relationship with her father change as the novel progresses? Find passages that illustrate how Mick and her father relate to one another.
5. What significant images appear in the novel? What images are associated with particular characters, and why?

Suggested Writing Assignments

1. Consider the theme of silence and communication and the effects of both on the development of the human person. Find a poem or a popular song that focuses on silence and/or communication and produce a piece of writing that expresses your reflection on the chosen poem or song. Your writing may be in the form of diary entries, an essay, a feature story for a magazine or newspaper, or in another form of your choosing.
2. Music plays a very important role in Mick's life. Think about what you might consider of equal importance in your own life—whether an art form, a sport, a personal goal, a hobby, or something else. Write an interview with yourself in which you use a question-and-answer technique to reveal the importance of this activity or goal in your life.
3. In essay form, compare and contrast the personal struggles of three characters from the novel. Identify the specific obstacles that make life difficult for each character, show how each character interacts with society, and analyze some of the major choices that the three characters make for themselves.

Sister Regina Noel, Villa Maria Academy, Malvern, Pennsylvania

THE HUMAN COMEDY

Villiam Saroyan's *The Human Comedy* is one of those small gems that, no matter how many times I reread it, brings loud laughs and quiet tears. Whether my students catch the laughter and tears from me or from the book, I'm not entirely sure. Anyway, they seem to like it, too. Maybe that's because it's refreshing to live for a while in a story that affirms and celebrates the indomitability of the human spirit, the strength of the family, the importance of work and of play, and the worth of the individual. It's a story that makes heroes of people like you and me, thus making it possible for all of us to be heroic when we need to be.

On the technical side, this novel is a wonderful diversion. Not only is the book brief and quickly read, but each chapter is a mere two or three pages. Thus the novel provides an example of a rather unusual form. It could be compared to Ray Bradbury's *Dandelion Wine* or to James Herriot's books; in certain respects it resembles James Agee's *A Death in the Family*. You and your students will be reminded of other stories, novels, and poems, I'm sure.

DISCUSSION QUESTIONS

1. It's as important for students to understand the particular time and place embodied in this book as it is for them to perceive its universal qualities. Discuss those aspects of the book that seem to belong to a certain time and place: attitudes toward the war—those of the people at home, those of the soldiers, those revealed through songs and newspapers of the 1940s; attitudes toward sex roles as displayed in Mrs. Macauley, in Bess and Mary, in the Ithaca Parlor Lecture Club; attitudes toward "foreigners" in a small California town. Describe and discuss forms of transportation and communication, jobs, peculiarities of language, activities in school and in sports, dating and boy-girl relationships, the structure of the

community—rather like one big family. Find clues in the novel that suggest the beginnings of changes in society.

2. Discuss the form of the novel, its point of view, and its style. Note the effects and limitations of the author's techniques. How would the story have been changed if Saroyan had used another point of view? More descriptive material? What threads help to form a whole cloth from the brief and separate chapters?

3. Discuss the literary allusions: for example, the allusion of the title to Dante's *The Divine Comedy;* names that allude to Homer's *Odyssey* (Homer, Ulysses, Ithaca). What is suggested by Marcus's name? Does Saroyan want his readers to make particular connections? Do these connections work?

4. Why does Saroyan use the telegraph office as the central setting for his novel? Where might a contemporary version of the novel be set?

5. Even though Matthew Macauley is dead, how is his influence still felt in the family? Discuss the concept of heroes depicted in the novel.

6. Comment on the value of music in the Macauley family.

7. Based on the novel, how did individuals view World War II? Have attitudes toward war changed since then? If so, how?

8. In what ways does life seem simpler then than now? More difficult?

9. Think about the kinds of prejudice shown in the novel: prejudice about class status, national heritage, mental capacity, the old or the sick or the very young, the ladies in the Bethel rooms, and others. Do these attitudes prevail today? Have they changed form or softened?

10. Mr. Spangler, Homer, and Mr. Grogan have broken the employment laws—Homer is too young, Mr. Grogan is too old, and Mr. Spangler overlooks both facts to hire them. Was he wrong? Were they? Was Mr. Spangler really doing them a favor (as it seems to the reader) by disobeying the law? What consequences, positive and negative, were there or might there have been?

11. Why does Saroyan allow Marcus to be killed in the war? It isn't fair! How does Saroyan suggest that there might be a longer-range justice or fairness? Is this a good enough trade-off for Marcus's life?

12. Speaking of fair, the novel generously dramatizes the adage that "No one ever said life is fair." Find examples. What conclusions do you draw?

13. How does being Valley Champion become symbolic in the novel?
14. According to the novel, what is happiness? Who possesses it? Can money buy it?

INDIVIDUAL AND SMALL-GROUP ACTIVITIES

1. Because each chapter is a separate scene and is built on dialogue, the novel invites acting out. Groups of students may select individual chapters or groupings of chapters to act out for the rest of the class.

2. Artists in the class might try their hands at a series of comic strips depicting events in the novel or creating their own adventures of "Homer at the Telegraph Office." Some might like to set Homer down in another place and time with a similar occupation and see what develops.

3. Stage a trial for Mr. Spangler after he has been charged with illegal hiring practices.

4   Research work laws and age. Why were such laws made? What are consequences, positive and negative, of such laws? Is the job market today losing the energy and creativity of youth as well as the experience and wisdom of older citizens by imposing age restrictions? Share your findings in a report, debate, discussion, or argumentative paper.

5. Locate popular songs, records, movies, radio programs, posters, art works and the like from the era of World War II. Bring your findings to class and lead a discussion on what these art forms suggest about the attitudes, values, and life style of that period.

6. Investigate Saroyan's life and writing. Report orally.

7. Compare the humor of today with that of the 1940s. Consider jokebooks, records or tapes of old radio comedies, movies, cartoons, or other sources you may discover. Draw conclusions and report orally.

8. Prepare a report based on interviews of people in their fifties about their memories of World War II. Are their memories similar to how the war is portrayed in the novel?

9. Prepare a speech in which your purpose is to persuade your audience (this class) to return to (or move forward from) the values dramatized in the novel.

WRITING ASSIGNMENTS

1. You are Mrs. Macauley. Write a series of diary entries responding to at least five events in the novel: for example, Ulysses' questions about when his father will come home or how you feel about Homer's working with Mr. Grogan. Remember to stay in character.

2. You are Mr. Spangler. Homer has reached age sixteen and is applying for a higher paying job. Write a letter of recommendation.

3. Organize a paper that makes clear how the scene with Simms-Peabody is funny and how it is serious. Why did Saroyan include this incident in the novel?

4. Go through the novel and list those times when Homer felt outraged. Is there a pattern to these situations as well as to the way Homer responds? Analyze what these incidents reveal about Homer.

5. Write a monologue similar in style to Homer's nose speech.

6. Make lists of the times you laughed and the times you wanted to (or did) cry during the reading of *The Human Comedy*. Were there occasions that made you laugh and cry at once? Examine your lists and draw conclusions on which to base an essay or a poem.

7. Explain Mr. Ara's confusion in adjusting to the American way of life. What does he want most for his son John? Why can't he give this to his son? Can you draw parallels with experiences of your own or with father-son relations that you have observed?

8. You are Mary. Write a letter to Marcus overseas.

9. At the end of chapter seven, Mrs. Macauley tells Homer that "schools are only to keep children off the streets, but sooner or later they've got to go out into the streets, whether they like it or not." What does she mean? Do you agree? Is her statement true for schools today? If you prefer, write an essay explaining what you believe the purpose of school should be. How could that purpose best be accomplished?

10. Write an essay explaining what you believe *The Human Comedy* says about life and about death. Use specific examples from the book to illustrate your points. The scene between the holdup man and Mr. Spangler is one example of finding meaning in life.

Beverly Haley, The Language Works, Fort Morgan, Colorado

TIPS FOR
THE HUMAN COMEDY

My eighth graders keep me honest. They don't allow me to cut corners or to get away with anything, and if they think I am wasting their time, they tell me so. But if they have a good time learning, they tell me that as well. Teaching under such close scrutiny has made me a careful planner and has improved the lessons I use.

The first time I taught *The Human Comedy*, I felt as though I had failed miserably, with the only high point being the showing of the movie after we read the book.

The second time, I added some interest to the lesson by requiring students to interview someone who was alive and on the home front during World War II. The information we shared helped students understand the setting as well as the actions and motives of the characters.

The third time I taught *The Human Comedy* was a genuine success. I included a writing assignment that was slightly different from most literature-based assignments--the writing of a human interest story.

I waited until students had read at least halfway through the book and gave the following quiz:

1. What extra or special duties involving Mr. Grogan does Homer have at the telegraph office?
2. What happens with Mrs. Sandoval?
3. What sort of person is Miss Hicks? Describe her.
4. What happens at the track meet?
5. What happens to Ulysses at Covington's Sporting Goods Store?

After we talked about students' answers to the above questions, I explained the writing assignment: to write human interest stories based on the reading. I passed around several human interest stories cut out of newspapers, and asked students to look at the stories and to talk about what made them different from headline news stories about current events. We agreed that human interest stories usually focused on admirable or inspirational qualities or achievements of one or more individuals, and that these stories used a more personal tone and were intentionally more subjective than regular news stories.

Next, I wrote on the chalkboard the following possible topics for human interest stories and asked each student to choose one:

1. Homer's wartime job
2. Mrs. Sandoval's telegram
3. Miss Hicks, history teacher to Ithaca
4. The Ithaca High School track meet; specifically, the 220-yard low hurdle race
5. Ulysses and the trap

We reviewed the importance of details telling *who, what, when, where, why,* and *how* in writing for newspapers. Students were to use their books to find details for their human interest stories, but they could make up additional information as long as it did not distort the story. Finished stories were checked for punctuation and spelling, revised, and copied over so that they were "ready for publication," that is, for showing to the rest of the class.

I've used this assignment successfully with several different reading assignments. Specifics of the assignment would vary, of course, according to the reading. For instance, when I assigned a television news report after the reading of "The Ransom of Red Chief," students were to write something that was brief but that showed an understanding of irony, a report suitable for "the lighter side of the news." An adaptation of this approach could be used to spice up the reading of almost any story or novel.

Travis E. Jackson, Suffern, New York

FUN, FOCUSED JOURNAL WRITING

For a long time, I wanted my classes reading *Catcher in the Rye* to write their *own* "Catcher." The candor and the vocabulary in the book seemed so much theirs already, and I thought that attempting the vividness of description, dialogue, and observation would be excellent practice for them. (I considered taking them *en masse* to a train terminal to practice observing people, but hesitated at such an undertaking.)

What finally emerged is the students' favorite writing project of the year; creating a "book" of observations. Since I don't want merely a diary or an unfocused journal, I assign a series of five or six writings, each with a focus that's general enough to elicit various responses. Prior to each assignment, I teach a writing skill and ask students to use what they have learned in the assignment. Rough drafts are due the following day, and I often use peer reviews so students can help each other with the assigned skill.

Following are some of the ways I have paired writing topics and skills. (Incidentally, each of these assignments is parallel to a scene in *Catcher in the Rye*.)

- Write a dialogue in which one or more of the participants reveals his or her true personality (preceded by a discussion of punctuation and indenting dialogue).
- Write about an incident that aroused a strong emotional response in you (preceded by a discussion of the importance of vivid verbs and by practice in substituting vivid verbs for bland ones).
- Describe your most memorable sensory experience within the past few weeks (preceded by a look at several vivid, well-written descriptions and class discussion of what makes them good).
- Describe various behaviors in a crowd scene (preceded by a discussion of imagery and alliteration).

- Write a character sketch that presents a memorable picture of a real or imaginary person (preceded by discussion of ways an author develops a character, such as describing the character's looks, mannerisms, the way the character speaks, and so on).

I usually write my own responses to the assignments as well; it gives students the feeling that we're working together, and provides an example for students of one possible way to respond to the assignment.

In our discussions of the book, we generally establish that Holden views the world with a negative, critical eye—through dark-colored rather than rose-colored glasses—so I usually ask students to determine what feeling of *theirs* predominates in their collection of completed writings. The titles they choose for their collections can then reflect that attitude. (Next year, I plan also to ask students to write a reflective piece at the end, directly commenting on the common thread or theme that they think they see in their work.)

Students copy their work over and put these good copies into final "book" form. The cover page or jacket is to be neatly done (and I encourage hand- or computer-done artistry), with a title that is both appropriate and "catchy." Before students take on this final step, I list actual book titles on the chalkboard, and we discuss what makes them catchy—whether alliteration, assonance, or the creation of a vivid image.

I make a big production out of the final turning in of students' books, which takes no effort at all since students put unusual care into this assignment and tend to be excited about finally turning in their books. As I read through the books, half of my reward comes from seeing students use their new skills, and half from seeing my students in a fresh, new way through the insights I find in their writing. I come away with deepened liking for my students as funny, sensitive, thoughtful, real people.

Carolyn Scott, Springfield Township High School, Philadelphia, Pennsylvania

THE OLD MAN AND THE SEA

This is the prose that I have been working for all my life . . .
—Ernest Hemingway, 1951

Ernest Hemingway hooked his first marlin in 1932—and generations of Americans have been hooked on the magnificent fish story he published twenty years after his catch off the coast of Havana. Deceptively simple in plot and lyric style, the novel deals with the classic verities of love and death, pride and humility. It stands as a miniature rival to *Moby Dick*, a parable complete with all the symbols, and an American artifact with a haunting thematic line: "A man can be destroyed but not defeated."

The work merits careful reading. It deserves at least twelve days of exploration--a probing of its form and content, of its idea and author. It also deserves instructional variety--reading and writing, teacher-and-student and student-and-student interaction, film and recording, fact and anecdote.

Suggested Schedule

Days 1–3	Introduction of the novel, including a discussion of Hemingway and the Nobel and Pulitzer Prizes, and time for in-class reading
Day 4	Explaining and assigning the position paper
Day 5	Discussing the Hemingway style and code through supplementary reading
Days 6–8	Prewriting, drafting, and anecdotal research
Day 9	Anecdote day
Day 10	Paper due with time for in-class proofreading

Days 11–12   Films: *Ernest Hemingway: Rough Diamond/The Old Man and the Sea*.

The first three days should provide a background for the novel as well as time for reading. Remind students that *The Old Man and the Sea*, first published in *Life* magazine, won the 1953 Pulitzer Prize and was instrumental in Hemingway's winning the 1954 Nobel Prize. You may wish to refer to W. J. Stuckey's *The Pulitzer Prize Novels*, pages 165-70, and to *American Winners of the Nobel Literary Prize*, edited by Warren G. French and Walter E. Kidd, especially pages 158-92, which include the Nobel Citation read at the ceremony in Sweden. Background information on Hemingway's Nobel Prize is also found in Carlos Baker's *Ernest Hemingway: A Life Story*, "The Bounty of Sweden," pages 525-29. These materials along with the Caedmon record/tape *Ernest Hemingway Reading*, which includes Hemingway reading his Nobel Address, will introduce the idea of awards and prizes as both delight and terror to authors. It is interesting to discuss awards at this point, since many writers both want and fear them. Fame and popularity can be time-consuming, distracting, even the kiss of death. John Steinbeck, for example, believed that little good material was written by Nobel winners after they received their awards.

Enterprising teachers will also want to make use of the genesis of the novel: "On the Blue Water" from the April 1936 issue of *Esquire*. (I have reprinted it in my *Writing Seminars in the Content Area: In Search of Hemingway, Salinger, and Steinbeck*, pages 105–108, a publication available from NCTE.)

The assignment given on Day 4 is crucial to the success of the entire project. Students are asked to begin work on a three-to-five-page typed paper in which they share their ideas about the novel with me and with each other. I call this a position paper because students are asked to limit their analysis to a single focus. This position is to be organized, supported by concrete detail, and mechanically sound. I offer the following position suggestions which students are free to accept, reject, or adapt.

1.   Why was this novel so important in Hemingway's winning the Nobel Prize?
2.   Is the Old Man just an old man or does he represent something else? Try to define him as a symbol.
3.   What is the function of the boy Manolin?
4.   Some see this novel as a parable. Review the meaning of *parable* and try to define your position in this way.

5. Take a key line, such as the last one in the book, and try to mold your position around that line.
6. Joe DiMaggio is mentioned in the novel more than once. Who was he? Could this lead to a position?
7. This novel won the Pulitzer Prize. Do some research on the prize and the historical period. Why do you think the book won the award during the Cold War?
8. Contrast or compare this novel with a Hemingway story, such as "The Big Two-Hearted River," or with the *Esquire* article "On the Blue Water."
9. Is Santiago a Code Hero? Can he be a man with "grace under pressure"?
10. Does this novel suggest a religious comparison? Is it a Christian story?
11. One critic said that the book is related to the "American Dream." Can you accept this? What does this mean?
12. Consider the ending. Is this story tragic or basically triumphant?

Day 5 is a time for reading aloud, for discovering and discussing Hemingway's style and for defining his world view (the Hemingway code). Instead of reading from *Old Man and The Sea*, I select one of the following stories to read aloud: "Ten Indians,""My Old Man,""A Clean Well-Lighted Place," or "The End of Something." Through discussion we piece together the Hemingway who believed in "grace under pressure," in the code of living with reality in a world of pain, of good and bad luck. Ask students, "If you had to write a paper on this story, what would be your position?" We go on to consider how we might document and organize that position based on the story we just read.

By Day 6 students have completed the novel, and we spend some time talking over how we write, how we get ideas. (What is the first thing you do when you write? Describe a successful paper that you once wrote; what made it successful?) Students also share the positions they are developing in their papers.

Since Hemingway was a highly autobiographical author and a charismatic human being, I ask students to do some simple research about the man behind the book. For this purpose I assemble in the classroom as much Hemingway material as I can from public, school, and personal libraries, from friends and colleagues and students, from old textbooks—original works, biographical and critical pieces, posters, newspaper and magazine clippings, recordings, picture files. Each student is asked to find an anecdote, a good story, to share with the class. On Day 9 students tell their stories about Hemingway's life as boxer, fisherman, hunter, bullfighting expert, expatriate; about his accidents, his wives, his children, his suicide, his parents, his high school years, his reaction to his prizes.

On Day 10, with time granted for in-class proofreading, the position papers are collected.

On Days 11 and 12 I sometimes show the 1958 Warner Brothers production of *The Old Man and the Sea* starring Spencer Tracy (Hemingway watched the filmmaking and later called it a waste of time) or the 1978 Centron film *Ernest Hemingway: Rough Diamond*, although I have also run *Rough Diamond* earlier in the schedule, about Day 3.

After I have graded the papers I choose three or four to share with the class. I ask the writer to read the paper aloud and then ask the other students to state the position of the paper. We take the class's formulation back to the author and ask if we have discovered the position. The author then has an opportunity to describe how he or she perceives the organization and support of the position. Now the paper is open for both positive comments and concerns about clarity and support.

After a dozen days, *The Old Man and The Sea* has been given its due: introduced, read, examined in terms of its author and his code, and explored through discussion, reflection. and writing. Students have heard it and seen it and felt it. (Sometimes I even offer students a chance to parody it.) In less than three weeks, everyone has found a friend--or maybe an enemy, the risk of all classics.

Brooke Workman, West High School, Iowa City, Iowa

SCOUT'S SCRAPBOOK

As an ongoing and review activity in connection with my sophomores' study of *To Kill a Mockingbird*, I ask students to compile a scrapbook that Scout Finch (or another character of their own choosing from the novel) might have kept. While they are reading the novel, students select items mentioned in the novel to include in the scrapbook. They find pictures of these items, or create facsimiles of them, and place them in the scrapbook. Items have included letters from Dill, Miss Maudie's Lane-cake recipe, B. B. Underwood's editorial, chewing-gum wrappers, Indian-head pennies, and articles about Tom Robinson's trial. Some students have even drawn the editorial cartoon of Atticus described in the novel.

Also, I encourage students to consider items which are not specifically mentioned in the novel but which are in keeping with Scout's character, items which she probably would have included. Some of the items students have created are announcements about the Halloween pageant, report cards, a news story relating the fire at Miss Maudie's, and Bob Ewell's obituary. Of course, many students draw "photographs" of the Finch family.

Finally, I have students write short essays explaining why they selected the items they included in the scrapbook and what these items reveal about Scout's character.

Students enjoy this activity. They produce more and better writing in creating items for the scrapbook than when I assigned similar topics to be done separately, perhaps because they feel they are self-assigning the work. I am pleased with the results and believe that students who invest themselves in the scrapbook project do better on more conventional assignments. Occasionally I have tried this activity with other novels, e.g., *Bless the Beasts and the Children*, *All Quiet on the Western Front*, and *Where the Lilies Bloom*, and have found it to be equally successful.

John Cebula, Glenbard West High School, Glen Ellyn, Illinois

PAPER BAG COLLAGES

had been struggling with *To Kill a Mockingbird* for four weeks, through the introduction of Scout and Jem; the Tom Robinson trial, verdict, and shooting; and the insights that Scout and Jem gain over the course of the novel. I was thoroughly enjoying the novel, relishing the bitter symbolism and the rich themes. But the other side of my desk might as well have been the other side of the moon, and my nodding sophomores were, at best, just enduring the unit.

Making literature "come alive" is a tough task for any English teacher. Although most of my white, middle-class, Wisconsin-born students had had little contact with other races and cultures, I felt there had to be a way to weave their lives into the lives of the Finches, the Radleys, and the Robinsons. I wasn't sure if many of my students had thought seriously about the issue of racial prejudice, so I decided on an idea which would be enjoyable in itself, help students get to know each other, and prompt discussion of the novel and of the theme of prejudice. What I tried with my students was certainly not earth-shattering, but it did seem to accomplish these goals.

I introduced the idea of the bag collage. In this exercise, students search through newspapers, magazines, or even photo albums at home to find pictures that symbolize different aspects of their personality. For example, one student cut out a picture of a tennis shoe from a catalog to represent her participation on the high school track team. Students may include small objects as well. Students sort their pictures and objects into two piles: those that represent aspects of their personalities that they often share with others and those that symbolize aspects that they may not share often or at all with others. I reassure students that they need not disclose their deepest, darkest secrets—only as much as they feel comfortable disclosing in this setting.

Once students have sorted their pictures and objects, I hand out paper grocery bags. They are to secure the items representing their outward personality traits on the outside of the bag; items representing their inner personality traits go inside the bag. For variation, some students have used other containers, such as shoe boxes or even pizza boxes. The paper bag seems to work best as it is easiest to carry or to hide in a locker.

I give students a week to think about and assemble their bag collages. I always make one, too. (Students love to find out that I'm really a soap opera addict!) Then we spend a day sharing the bags with each other as a class. Each student is encouraged, but not required, to share a collage. Once the exercise gets going, very few students decide not to.

As students reveal hidden aspects of themselves, they realize that not all facets of their personalities or lifestyles are readily apparent. Students often find that their classmates are more complex than they appear on the surface, that they have been wrong in their assumptions about their classmates' interests or talents, and that they have unsuspected things in common.

After we finish sharing the bag collages, I ask students to comment on this activity, writing their remarks on the board. Then I ask them what the bags have to do with *To Kill a Mockingbird*. Invariably students begin to talk about prejudice—about drawing conclusions about people based on outward appearances, about the inaccuracy of these conclusions, about prejudice within the school community, and about the symbolism and prejudice in the novel.

As our discussion winds down, I ask students to prepare a written example of what a paper bag collage might look like for some of the characters in the novel. (If time allows, this step could be expanded to help students more fully examine the characters in the novel.)

Students begin to discover each other and themselves in this short activity, and, though it's just a start, it also makes us more aware of our tendency to prejudge others. Its use shouldn't be limited to *To Kill a Mockingbird*; it could be an enjoyable way to prompt discussion and writing about any novel.

Rochelle Ohnesorge, Mosinee High School, Mosinee, Wisconsin

To Kill a Mockingbird

PREWRITING ON THEME

This year, after my ninth-grade classes read Harper Lee's Pulitzer Prize winning novel, *To Kill a Mockingbird,* and saw the movie, I used the following prewriting activities to focus students' attention on theme and prepare them for subsequent writing assignments.

I first asked students to form small groups to identify and discuss the key themes of the novel. When we came back together as a class, the groups presented their major points concerning themes in the novel. I wrote these points on the chalkboard and allowed some time for general discussion and clarification of the novel's themes. Examples of the themes (in italics) and general comments suggested by my students are listed below.

- The *injustice* manifested in Tom Robinson's false arrest, his trial, and the outcome, an unfair conviction. Closely related is the confusion that people experience when justice is destroyed by prejudice.
- The effects of *prejudice* and *discrimination,* which are kept alive through fear and ignorance, upon individuals, society, and the processes of the law. Racial prejudice is foremost in Maycomb, but class prejudice and the sexist treatment of women are also characteristic of this restrictive society.
- The *moral and emotional growth and maturation of Scout,* as a result of events taking place in the novel, from a state of naive innocence to a state of tolerance, enlightenment, and experience.
- The concept of *moral courage versus cowardice,* which is reinforced in the novel through a number of situations where characters' inner strength is challenged.

During the next class period, I had the class look at the novel's vocabulary, again in small groups. I divided the book into several parts and had each group choose a part of the book to work with. I explained that students were to skim the portion of the text that their group had chosen and were to select at least five words which described, suggested, or supported the key themes of the novel identified on the previous day.

After giving the groups time to complete their choice of words, I had each group present their words to the class. Students' selections, which I copied on the chalkboard, included such words as *abuse, courage, cruel, discrimination, prejudice, tormented, unfair,* and *wisdom.* I asked students to explain how their words related to a key theme of the novel and to give examples of events or situations described in the novel to support their selection.

Next, I used a variation of Dale D. Johnson's *semantic associations* strategy, which encourages students to realize that words are part of interrelated semantic networks. I asked the class to vote for the one word from our list that they would like to explore. The majority voted for *abuse,* a timely choice considering that abuse in many different forms is a societal problem much discussed in the past decade. I erased all of the words on the board except for the word *abuse,* around which I drew a circle. I asked students to brainstorm words that were suggested by or associated with the word *abuse,* and I recorded students' ideas on the board.

We discussed any words or phrases that students had questions or comments about, and then I asked students to scan our list and look for patterns of meaning or interrelatedness. I asked students to be especially sensitive to connections between words and the themes from *To Kill a Mockingbird* that we had discussed earlier. As students indicated connections between words, I drew lines joining the words. The result was the creation of the semantic map on page 187, which we then examined and discussed as a class.

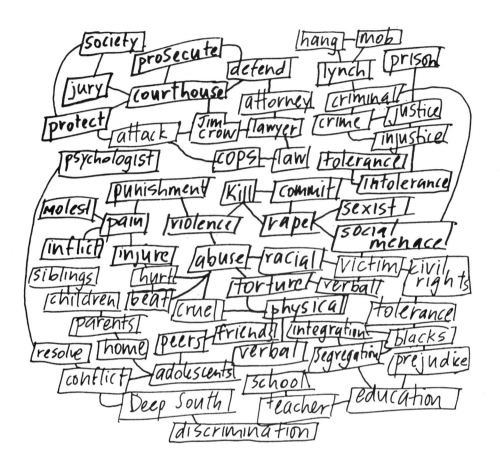

Bernice A. Hall, Denver, Colorado

DEVELOPING MATURITY THROUGH RESPONDING TO LITERATURE

Empathy is an ingredient essential to maturity. But until we accept the fact that we are all individuals with our own personal weaknesses, our subjectivity can make it difficult for us to empathize with others and to understand their actions. A worthy goal, then, is to engage students in activities that will open their eyes to individual differences and give them an occasion to develop compassionate discernment.

To Kill a Mockingbird is one appropriate vehicle for teaching individuality. I use prereading, core-reading, and postreading activities. Activity 1 (prereading) employs "sentence stubs" to jolt students into recognition of the various opinions and attitudes toward given situations. The "sentence stubs" or incomplete sentences can be written on the board or overhead for students to complete according to their personal experiences or preferences.

Some possible sentence provokers are listed below. These sentences address some of the issues found in *To Kill a Mockingbird*, and the responses will provide students with some insights into their own belief systems.

Activity 1

1. If my best friend began socializing with a social outcast, I would . . .
2. If I lived next door to someone who others thought was violent, I would . . .
3. If my friend used poor table manners while eating at my home, I would feel . . .
4. If my parent(s) were older than my friends' parents, I would feel . . .

5. If someone I care for were trying to conquer an addiction (e.g., food, alcohol, tobacco, drugs, etc.), I would feel . . .

After students have completed Activity 1, they share their responses and note the varying viewpoints that emerged. By giving special attention to those attitudes nurtured by society, I try to help students to see how environment shapes our conceptions of others. With this new understanding, students begin to read the novel.

Midway through the reading, I use Activity 2. In this core-reading activity, each student selects a situation in the novel that reveals varying attitudes or beliefs concerning others. Students are asked to compose a brief paragraph in which they reflect on a particular character's motivation in a given situation.

For example, Atticus's decision to stay outside of Tom Robinson's cell in order to protect his client from a lynch mob is motivated by his sense of justice and a wish to ease Tom's fear of violence. A student selecting this situation might briefly discuss what part society has played in the formation of Atticus's attitude. Another typical student paragraph might focus on Atticus's conversation with Scout concerning Scout's conflicts with her teacher and another student; the student author might explore the motivations behind Atticus's strong sense of fair play.

At the completion of Activity 2, students locate their "core sentence" or "center-of-gravity" sentence, using the technique described in *Writing*, by Elizabeth and Gregory Cowan (Scott, Foresman, 1980). To do this, each student examines his or her paragraph and locates a sentence that pinpoints the external or internal influences that prompt the character's behavior. For instance, the author of the second student paragraph mentioned above would be looking for a sentence that helps to explain why Atticus discourages Scout from prejudging people. In this case, the sentence selected as a "core sentence" might be one stating that Atticus's personal belief in human rights and his experience as an attorney have motivated him to advise Scout to refrain from judgmental arrogance when she has not been "inside the skin of another."

This activity reinforces the connection between the causes and effects of individual actions, allowing students to comprehend the complexities behind a person's actions and appreciate the significance of incentive.

A valuable side effect of this exercise is students' realization that although many outside sources may affect our volition, each individual alone must face the consequences of his or her decisions. *To Kill a Mockingbird* reinforces this principle elegantly.

At the completion of the novel, Activity 3 (postreading) focuses on the understandings and sensitivities cultivated by the students during this study. Students are assigned to write a dialogue between a senior and an incoming freshman in which the older student imparts advice about how one should respond to and coexist with peers, parents, and teachers during the next four years. The insight students have gained can then be passed on to the freshman English teachers to be shared the following year. What better way for students to learn tolerance and respect for others than through the encouragement of their peers?

Sally Reisinger, Klein Forest High School, Houston, Texas

Homer According to Morrison

A COMPARATIVE APPROACH TO THE *ODYSSEY*

Several years ago, the English department at the school where I teach decided to drop Homer's *Odyssey* from the freshman curriculum where it had been traditionally taught. The freshman teachers felt strongly that the epic was far too difficult a work to be dealt with by 14-year-olds: the length was seen as prohibitive, the language intimidating, the students' mythological background too scanty, and the entire experience so negative as to destroy Homer forever. Although I hated to see the work disappear from the curriculum, I was not ready to give up any of the works which I was teaching at the junior and senior levels and substitute Homer. I did find its disappearance a loss, however, particularly with my advanced placement students, who begin the year in September with a careful study of

Aeschylus's *Oresteia*. I found myself alluding to a Homer of whom they were totally ignorant; to a Trojan war which had no meaning for them beyond a vague image of a wooden horse—or a USC football game; and to an Odysseus who, at best, evoked images of a writhing Kirk Douglas tied to the prow of a Graeco-Hollywood vessel.

Then I discovered Toni Morrison's *Song of Solomon*.

For those who may not have read it, this prizewinning novel (it won the National Book Critics Circle Award for Fiction in 1978) recounts the story of a 20th-century American black, Milkman Dead, who sets out to discover his family history and in so doing discovers himself. Thematically, the novel is tied to the *Odyssey* in its evocation of a hero whose fullest identity is realized only after he has passed through a cycle of adventures which brings him "home." On a metaphorical level, Morrison's novel includes several adventures paralleling those of Odysseus: a trip to the world of the dead (Homer's Hades gives way here to a cave whose physical characteristics are analogous in many ways to those described in the epic); a visit to the realm of Circe (the island here is a rotting antebellum mansion inhabited by a wizened old woman who surrounds herself with Weimaraners; the alternately enchanting and revolting crone is named Circe, the only explicit Homeric parallel we find in the novel); a ritual baptism and "stripping down" of a protagonist, recalling Odysseus' arrival in the kingdom of Nausikaa; and several characters who recall key figures within the epic. Of these, the most striking parallel is afforded by the captivating Pilate, an androgynous, navel-less, protean figure who—like Athena—serves as Milkman's principal "helper" in discovering his identity and roots.

Aside from its link with the *Odyssey*, *Song of Solomon* is a highly readable book which virtually all of my 17-year-olds have enjoyed. My tactic has been to assign it to my advanced placement students as summer reading, along with the *Odyssey*. I ask students to give special attention to Books X and XI, where the parallels with Morrison's novel are particularly apparent. Before the summer begins, I alert them to the fact that we will focus on archetypal criticism in our discussion. Thus, they are reading *Song of Solomon* with a view toward finding its links with Homer, and they are reading Homer as a work whose characters and themes are as relevant for 20th-century America as they were for ancient Greek civilization. This lends an immediacy to the epic which is perhaps too often lacking in our teaching of it. It also gives students a broader and more meaningful context against which to discuss both works. Much class time is devoted to pulling out the various Homeric archetypes and finding their counterparts in Morrison; discussion takes on an almost detective-like quality at times and is very exciting for an advanced-level class.

In addition to discussion, I generally assign a paper in which students must discuss one or more of the similarities which we have found particularly interesting. Topics might look like this:

1. In Morrison's Pilate, one finds a character reminiscent of Athena, the figure who—more than any other—helps Odysseus to return home. Discuss specifically how Pilate resembles Athena, and how she aids the protagonist in his journey.

2. The theme of homecoming is central to the *Odyssey*. Explain how Morrison has adapted this theme in *Song of Solomon*.

3. The mysterious, ambivalent character of Circe is pivotal to the action in both the *Odyssey* and *Song of Solomon*. Describe the essence of this ambivalence, and state how the character helps catalyze action in each work.

4. Look at Joseph Campbell's monomyth diagram from *Hero with a Thousand Faces* (Princeton University Press, 1968) and discuss how Odysseus and Milkman reenact the heroic cycle of adventure. Identify clearly the "call to adventure," "threshold of adventure," "tests," "helpers," "elixir," and so on.

5. Consider the character of Elpenor, the unburied sailor whose restless soul Odysseus encounters in the Underworld and promises to bury. Discuss how Morrison resurrects the motif of the unburied body and its anguished soul in her novel.

The list is obviously endless. Perhaps a better idea would be to ask students to create a list of essay topics rather than write the essay itself, thereby forcing even more critical thinking--and reducing the paper load in the process!

Whatever the particular written assignment, the fact of having read the two works as a pair gets us right to the heart of each in short order. Students come away from the exercise with an appreciation for the eternal quality of Homer's work and with a heightened understanding of Morrison's novel. And I come away with a class whose enlarged frame of reference is more prepared to take on the challenge of Aeschylus.

Constance Hines Solari, Sacred Heart Preparatory School, Menlo Park, California

PATTERNS IN TONI MORRISON'S NOVELS

Toni Morrison's *Song of Solomon* won the National Book Critics' Circle Award for fiction in 1977, and when I read it that year I was struck by two things: the force with which it heightened my awareness (cliché, but true) of the black consciousness and the rich interweaving of Biblical and other images which created its meaning. Later, when I read *Tar Baby* (1981) and searched out her earlier *Sula* (1973), I was impressed by the patterns in all three novels and with their individual and cumulative effects. I wanted to discuss them with older high school classes ready to handle complex social issues (black vs. white, man vs. woman) and literary devices such as structure and pattern.

I had taught "Critical Reading" to general education students at Brigham Young University in which one unit emphasized concepts of structure. This unit introduced such questions as "What is the main idea of any piece of writing?" and taught that to find the main idea, a critical reader had to ask certain other questions: "What ideas (words, kinds of words) are repeated throughout the piece?" "Why is this (paragraph, episode, word) here, in this particular spot?" "What words (ideas) contrast with other words (ideas)?"

During this unit I also taught mapping, an exercise in drawing ideas presented in a work and using arrows or lines to show their relationships. Maps answer another important structural question: "How do the individual (words, sentences, paragraphs) relate to the piece of writing as a whole?" Students were challenged and intrigued, and a bit later I found Morrison's three novels, separately and together, proved helpful in teaching these concepts in high school.

All three books deal with relationships--between two people in particular and between one of the two people and his/her family as a secondary concern. *Sula*'s two main characters are women. Both have somewhat questionable backgrounds, and they are alike in other ways, too,

193

but they follow different paths as they become women. Sula chooses to leave the community, and when she returns she defies its mores and destroys its unity. Nel chooses to marry and build her own family within the community; even when Sula takes her husband, Nel continues to behave in traditional ways, visiting the sick and otherwise caring for community members. When at the end of the book Sula's aunt accuses Nel of being just like Sula, Nel is terribly disturbed but convinced that this is true in some fundamental ways, and she weeps for their damaged friendship.

In *Song of Solomon,* the two major characters are men. Milkman Dead is the unwanted but comfortable son of a wealthy black; his friend Guitar, not so comfortable, belongs to a secret society whose goal is to kill an innocent white for every innocent black murdered by white terrorists. Guitar needs money, and Milkman needs a purpose. Believing he can find gold because of a story his aunt told him, Milkman sets off to find his fortune, promising Guitar a share. At the end they meet in a death struggle; Milkman has found not gold but his ancestors, and Guitar believes Milkman has deserted him and hates him for it.

The two protagonists in *Tar Baby* are a black man and a black woman. Jadine has been educated in Paris and works as a chic and much sought after model. Son ("the only name that ever mattered" among all the names on his driver's licenses, army discharge papers, and other IDs) is from a Florida slum town called Eloe and has nothing but contempt for wealthy whites who have made Jadine's life possible. They fall in love on an island in the Caribbean, travel to New York where he is uncomfortable and to Eloe where she is uncomfortable, and then split up. At the end he is back on the island searching for her, aware that he does not want to live without her.

There are other similarities among these novels besides the plot pattern of two protagonists who are really two halves of one person struggling to resolve differences and experiencing violence and pain in the process. The two main characters in each novel have widely different perceptions of their responsibilities to families and communities, though both are deeply committed to these institutions. In all three novels, messengers from the past play an important role, and in all three, scriptural and folkloric songs, names, and stories influence the protagonists' lives.

I try to elicit awareness of these similarities as I teach these novels, and then I ask, "Can you figure out from all these patterns what Toni Morrison is trying to say through each book and through all three books?" If the students come up with something about the responsibilities of individuals to their past and future, about the orientation of black culture, or about the conflict between the good things in the materialistic modern white American culture, I feel I have helped them identify the significance of these novels for their own lives.

I would love to teach all three novels to an entire class, requiring every student to read each book. This takes time and energy a high school class generally doesn't have; what works better is to have the class divide into three groups, each taking one novel and presenting a discussion to the rest of the class. To make sure the three discussions lead somewhere positive, I have each group choose a member who will organize the presentation of their ideas to the rest of the class. Sometimes this person simply delegates, but there needs to be someone in charge. Next I tell them I will require a written report from everyone about the success of the group effort. Emphasizing that this is not just a tattle sheet, I ask, "Did everyone contribute something? Did you learn from the other group members? Did they help you understand the novel better?" Then I give each group the same set of questions:

1. What happens in the story? Summarize the plot.
2. Choose one or two words used repeatedly throughout the novel and tell how they change or grow in meaning or in importance from the beginning of the story to the end.
3. How do you feel at the end? Is everything resolved? What kind of epilogue would you write?
4. What does the novel say about blacks? Is it true, in your experience?

As students talk over these questions and then present them before the whole class, everyone begins to see patterns emerging. We then do a project on the history and influence of a local tradition or nursery rhyme or saying. This project generates enthusiasm--if there were time for only one activity based on Morrison's work, this would be it.

Written exercises always include a map of the books. Although forms and details on the maps may vary from student to student, the main ideas and major subheadings should be basically the same. Showing these maps as part of the group presentations helps the whole class see plot and theme patterns more clearly. (I recommend *Critical Reading* by Hansen, Herlin, and Marrott, available from BYU Press, Provo, Utah 84602, for more on mapping.)

I also have students write on one or more of these ideas:

For *Sula:* (a) Do you have a friend who is like you in many ways but also different? Write a paper in which you envision your two futures. (b) Suppose you left your town for ten years and then returned. Write an article for a newspaper or magazine from your new point of view. (c) Write a series of letters between two friends who have shared childhoods and high school years but haven't seen each other now for ten years.

For *Song of Solomon:* (a) Tell about the effect of your immediate family on you. Would you like to know more about your ancestors? What kind of effect do you suppose they have on your life? (b) What's in a name? Tell about someone, real or imagined, whose name is unusual or was given for what you consider a peculiar reason and tell about the effect of that person' s name on his or her life. (c) Make up a story about the origin of a nursery rhyme or game song.

For *Tar Baby:* (a) What is a tar baby? Why is that the title of the book? Do you think it's appropriate? What other name would you give it? (b) Why do you think Michael is in the book? If you were Ondine, would you have kept his secret—or, rather his mother's? (c) Write Valerian's journal for the period covered in the novel, and then write Sydney's.

By the time we're done with this unit, most students are amazed how much they can say about Morrison; our final exercise involves projecting her next novel's plot and structure, theme and images. If you teach a mature group of high school students ready to face some social and literary issues well united, try Toni Morrison on them. You may all come away more socially and literarily aware.

Julie J. Nichols, Brigham Young University, Provo, Utah

Barbara Kingsolver's *The Bean Trees*

STUDENT INTERACTION WITH CHARACTERS AS A MEANS FOR PERSONAL GROWTH

This strategy concerns Barbara Kingsolver's poignant novel, *The Bean Trees,* which I use with eleventh- and twelfth-grade contemporary literature students.

The Bean Trees serves as an excellent catalyst for a variety of activities that can meet the objectives of a curriculum stressing Reader Response, multicultural, and gender issues while simultaneously highlighting student talents and insights.

Successful classrooms are increasingly student-centered, and a Reader Response approach lends itself beautifully to this environment. Furthermore, the interaction students are able to have with the very credible characters in *The Bean Trees* fosters personal maturation and growth.

The Bean Trees chronicles the journey and adventures of a young woman named Taylor Greer, who leaves her Kentucky hometown in search of self and personal freedom. The unexpected responsibility of a Cherokee toddler, whom she later names Turtle, is only one of many surprises Taylor encounters along the roads of her travels. When Taylor and Turtle finally settle in Arizona, Taylor befriends Lou Ann Ruiz, Maggie, and refugees Esteban and Esperanza. These characters collectively search for freedom, a sense of belonging, and identity. Together they make many self-discoveries and find fulfillment in the love and support they share with one another.

I begin study of the novel with several personal response exercises which double as prereading activities. One response exercise includes word association. I ask students to write a list of word associations for the word "refugee," and then to write a one-paragraph description of a refugee. If they want to, students may also draw their impressions of what a refugee looks like.

In class, we then talk about their impressions and about where their ideas and images originated—whether from radio or television news reports, family history, Hollywood films, or other sources. From this, we move on to explore why people would want to flee or run away from their homes. With a partner, students construct a list of eight to ten reasons why someone would want to leave or run away from something. In class, we cross-reference similar items that students find. I remind them to think about the characters when they are reading and the reasons why the characters want to "escape" their given predicaments.

I also want students to explore myths and facts about American Indians. Working in groups, they create lists of words, phrases, and images that they associate with "Indians." We share these lists as a class, discuss where these images come from, and try to identify stereotypes such as "feathers in hair," "painted faces," or "lives in a teepee." One side benefit of the discussions that arise is that they help students to examine their preconceptions about other people and to realize that some of their impressions about other groups are likely to be opinion and not fact.

After we have constructed these elemental foundations for study of the novel, I introduce the format for keeping a Character Dialogue Journal (similar in format to a Double Entry Journal). Students hold a sheet of paper horizontally and fold it into three columns. Each column has a different purpose. After students have read a given assignment or completed a segment of the novel, they use this journal to respond to their reading in a variety of ways.

In the first column, *Character Questions/Comments,* students write directly to the characters and create questions or comments they have for the characters. This column lends itself well to prompting class discussions. The second column is *Questions/Comments* for the author. Sometimes these insights help clarify literary elements that individual students struggle with. They also help keep me in touch with student reading. The third column, *I Feel . . .,* helps students follow their emotional reactions to any given character and offer input to character behavior, actions, or outcomes. Identification with characters tends to lead to a closer reading of the novel.

A sample Character Dialogue Journal might look something like the one on page 201.

This journal allows students to become actively involved in the lives of the characters. Furthermore, it serves as a prompt for a number of activities.

One such activity is prompted early on in the reading of the novel. After approximately seventy-five pages of reading, students have been exposed to a handful of characters. They are asked to share their best questions and comments in a small group setting. Halfway through the class period, I ask a group spokesperson to write three of the best questions/comments on the chalkboard while another group member writes them on a ditto which is circulated about the room. Together we look at the questions. The following day, I hand out the student-generated worksheet. I then allow students twenty minutes to respond as fully as they can to any five of the twenty or so created questions. This enhances their understanding and interaction with specific characters.

Another activity that grows from the Character Dialogue Journal is to place students in groups which represent the characters. Primary characters include: Maggie, Taylor, Lou Ann, Turtle, Esteban, and Esperanza. Each group is responsible for creating a list of ten known facts for their character and creating a minimum of three questions for each of four of the five other characters.

The next day in class, the groups "become" their characters for a question-and-answer session. During the first half of the class period, each group takes a turn in asking questions. Then in the second half, the floor is open to any questions addressed to a "character." I ask groups to decide which group they think was most convincing in its character role, and to jot down a brief explanation as to why they chose that group. I collect the lists of facts, questions, and explanations to use for assessment.

The final activity to be used later or at the close of the reading involves five volunteers who represent the five main characters. Students at their desks are asked to create two questions for each character. Again, an organized question-and-answer period takes place, followed by an open floor question-and-answer session. Characters are allowed to comment and question each other; this adds to their believability.

I check the Character Dialogue Journals at the midpoint of the novel, and students receive feedback periodically through sharing with partners at the beginning of class. Journals are also collected at the end of the novel. If desired, the questions can be used to generate a student take-home exam which involves Reader Response answers.

At the close of the reading, students can be asked to compose an in-class essay in which they discuss at length the character who most affected them and why, incorporating comments from their journals.

A number of enrichment activities are possible, including a character diary, character portrait, character magazine, or a three-dimensional representation of their favorite character. Another option is a partnering of students in which they follow a script to answer and possibly debate one of the following topics: Taylor's success as a parent, Mary Lou's success as a parent, the actions of refugees and the students' support of or disagreement with various reasons for leaving one's country. Students may present their debates to the class or tape record them for later review by the teacher.

Of the countless pieces of literature by women authors which can be taught in the classroom, Barbara Kingsolver's *The Bean Trees* is a work that provides many possibilities for discussion and writing, and one that opens the windows of the students' minds and allows us, as teachers, a peek inside.

Kristen Klugh-Carter, Upper Darby High School, Upper Darby, Pennsylvania

Sample Character Dialogue Journal

CHARACTER COMMENTS/ QUESTIONS	AUTHOR COMMENTS/ QUESTIONS	I FEEL . . .
Why does Missy/Taylor want to get away so badly?	Why does Kingsolver write all this stuff about the Hardbines?	Missy/Taylor's mom is great and supportive: (p. 5) "Mom says trading her husband for me was the best deal . . ."!
Missy/Taylor's mom seems pretty cool!	I like Kingsolver's descriptions: (p. 10) "She (mom) acted like it was the moon I had just hung up in the sky and plugged in all the stars. Like I was that good."	
Why does Missy/Taylor insist on dressing "memorable"?		
I don't understand Taylor's "head rights" regarding the Cherokee Nation. What does this mean to her?	What is the importance of 1-800-THE-LORD?	I feel Taylor is confused. She seems like she's trying to find something but she's not sure what she's looking for.
Why doesn't Taylor resist taking the child? I remember *you* didn't want to end up pregnant and with kids at the beginning of the story.		
	I like the way she describes people so I can picture them!	I feel so sorry for the Cherokee baby—I think Taylor will be good for her.
I'm not sure whether to like Esteban or not.	Why are all the male characters (Hardbines, fathers, etc.) portrayed as deadbeats?	I feel this is a girl's/woman's book because the women rule the whole plot!
	I can't picture Lee Sing as well as the other characters.	Lou Ann is so lame! She needs to get some self-esteem!
Esteban, do you really like Taylor? What type of relationship do you want with her? I think your wife, Esperanza, is *so* nice!	Where do you want to go with the character of Esteban? Should we admire him or hate him? I feel a little of both, but I can't make up my mind.	Maggie reminds me of Taylor's mom. I feel they are both "saviors" in the story.
Turtle, why do you love vegetables and gardens so much? Did you see planting when you lived on your reservation?	Why do you make Turtle's first words *vegetables*.	I feel Taylor and Esteban are falling in love with each other.
Taylor—how does it make you feel when Turtle calls everyone else "Ma?" This would upset me.	Why do you describe the flowers and gardens so much? Is it symbolic?	
	I like the fact that you don't focus on Turtle's abuse or abusers. I am glad I'm finally reading a story that celebrates someone's victory over such troubling things.	
		Taylor has discovered so much about herself by the end of the story. I feel a lot of admiration for her!

Barbara Kingsolver's *Animal Dreams*

ENCOURAGING THE STUDY OF CONTEMPORARY LITERATURE

B arbara Kingsolver is a contemporary American woman author whom I have found to be very well received by my high school English students. Ms. Kingsolver offers the kind of stories students identify with and the kind they are very willing to discuss.

When I first considered using Ms. Kingsolver's work, I hesitated because she is not part of the canon of works normally taught in high school. I wondered about how she would stack up against classic authors like Hemingway, Camus, Dickens, Steinbeck, the Brontës, and others. But my desire to teach a modern novel and one which contained contemporary issues outweighed my initial hesitation. And after all, Charles Dickens was a "bestselling" author in his own time, and no one anticipated he would be read and studied so extensively in our time. In addition, I was glad to find in Kingsolver's novels strong female protagonists, which I felt my students would all benefit from.

The book I chose to use is *Animal Dreams*. (Kingsolver's other two novels are *The Bean Trees* and *Pigs in Heaven*.) *Animal Dreams* is set in a small mining town in Arizona called Grace; it is the story of Codi and Hallie Noline, their father Homer, and the interplay of family history in the development of self-identity. Told in the first person through the troubled eyes of Codi, the story is about beginnings, family, hometowns, lost loves, found love, self-discovery, life's mistakes, community identity, ecological disaster, and the myths we tell ourselves and others in order to be whole. In sum, it is about many of the problems our students face today and are struggling so hard to understand. I believe this book helps them to come to terms with many issues. Yet this is an adult book which handles the conflicts as adults would handle them; it is not an adolescent literature novel.

In beginning the novel study, the books are handed out a week to two weeks in advance and the class understands it is to be read in its entirety by the time discussion begins. My students already keep a response journal for everything we read, so reminding them to continue the journal for *Animal Dreams* is not a surprise. Because the book deals with the main character starting her life over by returning to her hometown, I suggest that students' first in-class journal response deal with "new beginnings/starting over," in whatever way this topic relates to them. They can address what it's like to be the new kid in school, moving to a new location, going through a new phase, or even what the future holds for them, what it will be like, and what they expect to find. This journal assignment generated a lot of discussion among my students, some of whose parents work for the local branch of a large computer company that often transfers its employees. These students can really relate to the trauma, the nervousness, the anxiety of moving. Also, because the students in this class were seniors and most if not all planned to attend college, they were able to anticipate what it would be like starting over at college and how they would handle it.

The first day's writing can be followed by discussion of the first part of the novel where Codi returns to Grace, her hometown, to start her first teaching job. Either just before or just after this discussion, I play Bruce Springsteen's recording, "My Hometown" (available on *Bruce Springsteen and the E Street Band Live 1975–85*) for the class and ask the students to respond in writing to the topic "My Hometown." Many kinds of response are possible. Students can describe prominent features and other specific details of their hometowns. If they are native to the area, they can write about the way in which they see their hometown now, how they saw it when younger, and how it has changed as they've grown up. Students who grew up somewhere else can write about "going home" and what it feels like to return to their hometowns. Students' responses to this topic are a natural lead-in to a discussion of Codi's feelings about returning to Grace, a town that does not hold many positive memories for her.

One of the areas we touch on in discussion is Codi's troubled relationship with her father, the town's only doctor. We move into exploring the interconnectedness of Codi, her father, and Hallie, her sister who never actually appears, and then I ask the students to paint a written portrait of their families, including a one- to two-sentence thumbnail sketch of each member of the family and his/her role or position in the family, including themselves. Next, I ask students to write about their relationship with each of the family members. The students may discuss conflicts in their own families if they wish, but this is wholly voluntary. The thinking and writing students do about their own families helps them to relate to the novel, which has at its heart family relationships. There is no attempt made to pry into sensitive areas, but if the students seem interested in further discussion on family relationships, I think it enhances the class's reading of the novel.

Problem solving and conflict resolution can be discussed at this point by relating the conflicts within the book to each other as well as discussing possible solutions. This includes a lively discussion of the helping forces and the hindering forces involved in each of the conflicts, both major and minor. For the hampering forces, students can list possible action steps which the character(s) can take to reach a resolution to the conflict. By examining the most likely steps the character would take, based on what they know about the character, the students also discuss characterization. The steps can then be placed into an overall plan and a sequence to the action can be determined.

Because the book is very personal and strikes the students as such, as prompts or warmups for the day, I ask them to pick something in the book that elicits a personal response. They describe their choice and explain why it elicits a personal response. I also ask my students to choose a line or phrase from the novel that says something to each of them. We share these and explain our choices.

The novel also deals with names and their importance. Codi, whose name is actually Cosima, puts a lot of credence in names. One of the students' assignments is for each student to write about his or her name, its origin, its meaning, what it says about him or her, any nicknames he or she has, and to answer this question: Given the opportunity to, would you change your name? This generated a very interesting discussion.

In concluding the novel, after much discussion of the usual elements, I ask the students to write a posthumous letter, from Codi to Hallie, that wraps up the conflicts of the novel. They are to try to write in Codi's voice and style, which is interesting for them since the novel is told in first person. They are to capture the relationship between the two sisters and to show that Codi has reached some kind of inner peace now that her sister has died and she (Codi) has come to accept herself. I plan to mail some of the best of these to Barbara Kingsolver, because students were so good at capturing Codi's voice and at offering insights into the characters and situations. I also ask my students to write a defense for using the book in the class, and every one of them so far has defended the book's use on the grounds of relevance, enjoyability, and quality.

This is a warm and multifaceted novel and one to which each of my students has been able to relate. Even though it is outside the usual canon of books taught in high school English, it is as important to the students and their situations as the works of Dickens, Twain, and Shakespeare. I thank Ms. Kingsolver for providing me a refreshing change of pace and for showing my students the possibilities in contemporary literature.

Jonathan Larson, Longmont High School, Longmont, Colorado

THE ART OF STORYTELLING IN LESLIE SILKO'S *CEREMONY*

As an introduction to Native American culture, I teach Leslie Marmon Silko's novel, *Ceremony* (1986), in my American novel class for college bound juniors and seniors. *Ceremony* incorporates the art of storytelling and the myths, rituals, and ceremonies of the Navajo and Pueblo Indians in the southwest United States. Silko writes, "You don't have anything if you don't have the stories" (Mitchell 1979, 28).

The narrative structure of the novel is a challenge for students because there are no chapter divisions. Silko uses both prose and poetic forms to tell the story of Tayo, a young half-breed Laguna Pueblo Indian who has lost his will to survive after suffering through the Bataan Death March and a Japanese prisoner-of-war camp. The prose sections provide the students with the events of Tayo's life before, during, and after World War II, while the poetic structures are the myths, legends, and chants of the Pueblo and Navajo tribes.

The difficulty in teaching *Ceremony*, however, is not in its narrative structure or its readability, but in students' lack of understanding of the Native American way of life. Therefore, I begin this unit with the following assignment. I give each student copies of the Cheyenne creation myth and the first three chapters of Genesis from the Bible. I emphasize that the material from Genesis is used as literature in this context. The students read these myths before the next class period and bring a list of differences between them using the following questions:

Who creates the universe?
How is the universe created?
How does each myth present the world and its inhabitants or the world view?

During the discussion, we develop a chart based upon the assigned questions on the chalkboard or overhead and list the differences. (See Figure 1.) I add to the chart the concept of time and space because my students are often mystified and confused by the movement of time in the novel. They complain that Silko jumps about from the past to the present and back again. Literary critic Paula Gunn Allen calls this "ceremonial time" in which "events are structured in a way that emphasizes the motion inherent in the interplay of person and event" (Allen 1986, 148). By using a circle and dividing Tayo's life into four time-periods and by continually reminding students that we are viewing time as cyclical rather than sequential, I help them comprehend why all the events in Tayo's life tie together. (See Figure 2.)

Throughout the novel, Silko weaves into Tayo's narrative the ancient myths of the Navajo and Pueblo tribes, their ceremonies, and rituals. Because Tayo is a half-breed who has neither training nor education in the Laguna way of life, he experiences profound alienation and despair. For Tayo and the students, these stories and traditions help "make the old ways understandable and relevant to the contemporary situation" (Mitchell 1979, 28). In the first four pages, Silko presents the Laguna creation myth, a ceremony, and a ritual. In the center of these are the myths or sacred narratives. For Native Americans, these stories concern the universe and the spiritual domain. They are didactic because they teach the history of the people, how to live, and how to survive. According to Allen, "myth is a story

Cheyenne: Native American	Genesis: Western Christian
1. Creator of the Universe: Maheo	1. Creator of the Universe: God
2. How the universe is created: All creatures share in the process of creation which makes all things sacred. For Native Americans, this is called the Sacred Hoop of Being.	2. How the universe is created: God is separate and has no creative assistance from his creatures. God is sacred.
3. World View: Creatures and people alike are given needs, so they can work together to solve common problems or attain common goals.	3. World View: The Christian universe is based upon separation and loss. In Paradise, God created the perfect environment for his creatures and people. When man and woman disobey God, they are exiled.
4. Nature: There is no separation of the natural or supernatural. All phenomena Native Americans witness within or outside of themselves are intelligent manifestations of the universe from which they arise.	4. Nature: The Universe is divided into two parts: the natural and the supernatural. Humanity has no real part in either, being neither animal nor spirit.
5. View of Time and Space: Space is viewed as spherical and time is cyclical. All points which make up the sphere of being have significant identity and function.	5. View of Time and Space: Space is viewed as linear and time as sequential. The linear model assumes that some points are more significant than others.

Figure 1. The Differences between Native American
and Western Cultures

THE PRESENT
- Harley/Tayo ride burro
- Curing Ceremony with Betonie
- Tayo meets Ts'eh
- Tayo finds Josiah's cattle
- spends summer with Ts'eh
- last witchery with Emo
- tells story to elders

BEFORE WWII
- early childhood with mother
- later childhood/teen
  years with Auntie
- Josiah and Mexican
  cattle deal
- Josiah and Night Swan
- Tayo and Night Swan

**TAYO'S TIME
ANCIENT TIME
(the myths)**

AFTER WWII
- Tayo in VA hospital
- Tayo at home with Auntie
- Scalp Ceremony
- Tayo stabs Emo

DURING WWII
- on Corregidor
- Bataan Death March
- Rocky dies
- Japanese Prison Camp

Figure 2. The Cyclical Nature of Time in *Ceremony*

of vision . . . a vehicle of transmission of sharing and renewal." It connects the past with the present. Silko's myths "show us that it is possible to relate ourselves to the grand and mysterious universe that surrounds and informs our being . . . . The mythic heals, it makes us whole" (Allen 1986, 116–17). Folklorist Carol Mitchell explains that by using the Laguna creation myth at the beginning of the book "Silko recreates the power and time of creation. The cosmic creation is the exemplary model of all life," and Silko hopes that it will restore the patient, Tayo. Mitchell also believes that the use of this myth is a "spiritual means by which the novelist is inspired in her creative work" (Mitchell 1979, 28).

Ceremonies are the ritual enactment of the myths, that is, the actual telling of the stories by the shaman or storyteller. Silko states,

I will tell you something about the stories,
[he said]

They aren't just entertainment.
Don't be fooled.

They are all we have, you see,
all we have to fight off
illness and death

. . . .

And in the belly of this story
the rituals and the ceremony are still growing.

(qtd. in Mitchell 1979, 28)

Finally, there are the rituals. These are the actual physical doing of what is told in the myths. The purpose of the procedure is to "transform something (or someone) from one state or condition to another" (Allen 1986, 103). The novel is a healing ritual which changes Tayo from a diseased state, one of isolation and despair, to one of health, encorporation with his people. I use a circle which places the myths in the center and the ceremonies and rituals around the edges. (See Figure 3.)

As the students read the novel, they identify these three traditions and discuss how they are used within the text. By using the circle, the students begin to see the connections among them and why they are central to Tayo's story.

Myth, ceremony, and ritual converge at the center of the novel. Tayo is sent by his family and village elders to Betonie, a Navajo shaman, to help him recover. Silko, through the character of Betonie, narrates the Coyote Transformation story in which Coyote steals a son-in-law away from his family. Coyote transforms himself into the son-in-law while the young man becomes Coyote. The family searches for their child, and when they find him, they must ask the four old bear people for help in bringing the boy back to normal. The ritual described in this story is the actual procedure that Betonie uses for Tayo. Betonie creates a sand painting for Tayo's ritual.

He [Tayo] sat in the center of the white corn sand painting. The rainbows crossed were in the painting behind him. Betonie's helper scraped the sand away and buried the bottoms of the hoops in little trenches

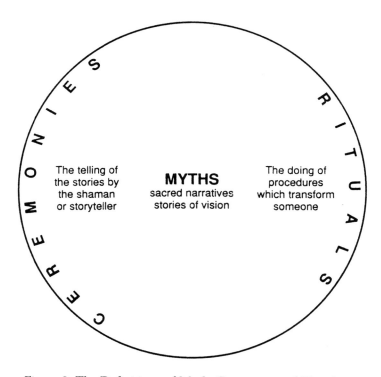

Figure 3. The Definitions of Myth, Ceremony, and Ritual

so that they were standing up and spaced apart, with the hard oak closest to him and the wild rose hoop in front of the door. The old man painted a dark mountain range beside the farthest hoop, the next closer, he painted blue, and moving toward him, he knelt and made the yellow mountains; and in front of him, Betonie painted the white mountain range. (141–142)

The hoops "represent a space so narrowed down that it is under ceremonial control, an area from which evil has been ritualistically driven and within which power has been concentrated" (Kingsolver 1990, 299). Tayo reenacts the mythological events, and when he is lifted through the hoops, he is symbolically freed from evil. Tayo then experiences a cosmic sense of the universe.

He took a deep breath of cold mountain air; there were no boundaries; the world below and the sand paintings inside became the same that night. The mountains from all directions had been gathered there that night. (145)

At the end of the ceremony, Betonie has a vision for Tayo. "Remember these stars," he said. "I've seen them and I've seen the spotted cattle; I've seen a mountain and I've seen a woman" (152). This concludes the *Ceremony,* and now Tayo must complete the ritual by seeing the stars, finding the cattle and mountain, and discovering the woman.

Ceremony is a complex novel, but its richness and texture provide students with an accurate depiction of Native American ways of life. Because Silko is a remarkable and accomplished storyteller, the students have no difficulty identifying or analyzing the theme of alienation. When they complete this unit, they come away with an understanding and appreciation for this culture. I ask the students to evaluate the novel.

> *Aaron:* This novel made me think about and question our Western traditions. This not only made me realize our wrongdoing but to detest it

> *Mary Beth:* This is the most spiritual book I have ever read. What an ending when Tayo refuses to fight Emo. I know Tayo will be at peace. That's comforting.

Barbara Kingsolver best states my hope for teaching *Ceremony* as we approach a new century: "The possibility that kids might one day grow up to be neither the destroyers nor the destroyed" (Kingsolver 1990, 299).

WORKS CITED

Allen, Paula Gunn. 1986. "The Ceremonial Motion of Indian Time: Long Ago, So Far." *The Sacred Hoop: Recovering the Feminine in American Indian Traditions.* Boston: Beacon. 147–54.

——. 1986b. "Something Sacred Going on Out There: Myth and Vision in American Indian Literature." *The Sacred Hoop: Recovering the Feminine in the American Indian Traditions.* Boston: Beacon. 102–17.

Mitchell, Carol. 1979. "*Ceremony* as Ritual." *American Indian Quarterly* 5 (Feb.): 27–35.

Bell, Robert C. 1979. "Circular Design in *Ceremony*." *American Indian Quarterly* 5 (Feb.): 49.

Kingsolver, Barbara. 1990. *Animal Dreams*. New York: Harper.

Silko, Leslie Marmon. 1986. *Ceremony*. New York: Penguin.

Nancy Gilderhus, Thomson Valley High School, Loveland, Colorado